The Face of True Love

The Face of True Love

By

N.J. Nash

Strategic Book Publishing and Rights Co.

Strategic Book Publishing and Rights Co.
12620 FM 1960, Suite A4-507
Houston TX 77065
www.sbpra.com

ISBN: 978-1-62212-905-8

ACKNOWLEDGEMENTS

This book is written for everyone who has ever suffered physical or mental abuse in their lives and has the scars to prove it. I would like to dedicate it to my first new grandson, Archie. My grateful thanks go to Joe Folkes, my boss' son, who helped me a great deal in understanding the ins and outs of the laptop. I hadn't got a clue, but I've learnt. Thank you.

"No, Daddy, no. It hurts. Please, don't hurt me Daddy, no, please. I'm bleeding, Daddy, no, it stings," she screams.

"You stupid little bitch, shut your mouth. Fucking little whore, just like your mother." And the whip comes down on her again, curling round her small body like a snake.

Vicky wakes in a panic; there are arms around her, holding her tight. She then realises that the arms are loving ones, and she is safe.

THE BEGINNING

Vicky Foster was just ten years old when her mother died. She got knocked down by a car whilst out getting medicine for Vicky, who was ill at home. Her father had been distraught and cried for days after it had happened. They had been a close, loving family, just the three of them. But then Vicky started to notice a change in him. He started drinking and staying out late, never spending any time with her at all. She grieved for her mother on her own; she missed her.

It was then that it started. At first he just kept her off school, telling the teachers she was being tutored privately, but she wasn't. He made her sit and do sum after sum so she could learn how his accountancy business ran, telling her that she would work for him and never go out to work anywhere else. It was hard for her, though, and she made mistakes often. She would get a slap round the head, or he would thump her and call her a stupid little whore like her mother, which she couldn't understand because he had loved her mother. The only time he was nice to her was in front of people, especially their longtime family friends Tony and Dolly Armstrong and their two sons, Eric and David. Vicky had known them all her life and they were the only family she knew, even though they weren't blood related, and she had practically grown up with Eric and David. They would see them often and stay there for long weekends; she loved it there because he would leave her alone. Every time they went to visit them he would make sure she had a clean dress on, but would warn her in no uncertain terms not to open her mouth, else she would pay for it later when they got home. She would get the occasional dig in the ribs while they were there, just to remind her. So she never said a thing.

One night he came home from the pub drunk and it was this night that he told her that he had brought her a present. Vicky was surprised, as he never gave her anything nowadays except a beating. He told her to open the box and when she did, she blanched. There it was, a long thick leather whip. "That's what you will be getting from now on if you don't do things right, you fucking little whore," he said in his drunken mumble. "Get out of my sight, you make me sick, it's your fault your mother's dead, you killed her." With that he fell onto the chair, but Vicky just ran up to her room and sobbed.

She was woken abruptly about two hours later, "Come on you little fucker, I want something to eat," he shouted at her as he pulled her off the bed by her arm. She noticed he was holding the whip, the long end circled round his hand. "Do you want me to try this out on you do you?" he snarled at her. She ran down the stairs as quickly as she could but he was right behind her. "Get me something to eat, bitch," he said. His face was right up to hers and she could smell the whisky on him.

"What do you want?" she whispered.

"Oh, fuck the food, you're fucking useless anyway. Get over there and stand facing the wall," he snarled.

Vicky did as she was told. She felt the pain before she heard the crack of the whip; she screamed in agony and collapsed to her knees. Then it came again and again. He was laughing at her, calling her everything, swigging his whisky out of the bottle with his other hand. The tears were rolling down her face; she was in agony. "No, Daddy, no. It hurts. Please don't hurt me, Daddy, please. I'm bleeding, Daddy, no, it stings," she screamed.

"You stupid little bitch, shut your mouth. Fucking little whore, just like your mother." And the whip came down on her again, curling round her small body like a snake. He collapsed in the chair and within minutes he was snoring.

She gingerly got herself to her feet. Her nightdress was ripped and covered in blood. She carefully took it off, and ran herself a warm bath. She didn't know what else to do; she was in agony and alone.

This carried on for the next seven years, getting worse and worse every time. He would beat her and whip her senseless. Her body was now scarred and battered but she couldn't do a thing; he had knocked everything out of her. Their house was up a remote driveway on its own, so they had no neighbours to hear anything and he knew it, and he told her if she mentioned anything to anyone he would kill her like she killed her mother. He had his reputation to think of, as everyone liked him and he was kind and generous with everyone. Except her.

She was now coming up to her eighteenth birthday; she had plans to get away then, as once she was eighteen he would have no hold on her. "Don't you get any silly ideas, bitch, will you, just because you're going to be eighteen. You will be nice and ripe then, won't you?" he said to her one night.

"What do you mean, ripe?" she asked.

He threw his head back, laughing. "Fucking stupid thick whore, ain't you. It means I will be able to fuck you. I could have been doing it for the last few years but I decided to wait till you were nice and juicy all over. And you are under my lock and key until you're twenty-one so I've got three years of nice ripe fucking to do. Nobody else will ever want you with a body disfigured like yours is," he said as he put his face in hers.

Vicky stepped back away from him but he grabbed the front of her dress, pulling the buttons off. "No Daddy, please, you're hurting me" she said as she tried to pull away.

"Good, bitch, you deserve to be hurt. And once you turn eighteen I can hurt you some more. Happy birthday for then, whore," he spat.

Vicky was more frightened than ever; her birthday was just two days away and she was stuck here for another three years. No way could she stand it; she had to get away somehow.

But with no money of her own and no way to get anywhere, what could she do?

Her birthday was here and she was in fear of her life. She knew and understood what he was going to do to her and she didn't know what to do, apart from try to fight him off, or kill him. That night he came in from the pub and he was in his element. "Come and give your Daddy some love and kisses, birthday whore," he sneered at her.

"Keep away from me, you bastard," she shouted at him.

His eyes opened wide, and he just stood and glared at her. "WHAT. Are you refusing me that nice ripe body on your birthday? Now, you should know better than that, bitch," he said as he grabbed her arm, his fingers biting into her flesh. She tried to pull away but he was strong; he pulled her back and slapped her face hard, making her see stars. Before she knew it he was on top of her on the floor, pulling at her clothes; his hand was up her dress pulling her knickers down, with his fingers trying to get to her. She managed to knee him in his groin and he rolled off her, holding himself and writhing in agony. "You've had it now, you fucking bitch" he said as he rubbed himself.

Vicky was up off the floor and ran up the stairs. She had to hide. As she ran she looked back and saw him stumble to his feet, still holding himself, and he grabbed the whip. "Fucking whore, get back here. I'm going to give you the beating of your life. Then I'm going to fuck you senseless, bitch. You can't hide, I'll find you," he shouted as he made his way to the stairs.

Vicky ran into his bedroom, as he wouldn't think to look for her there; she hid behind the big armchair. She could hear him cursing and banging about, thumping everything in his way. Then, suddenly, he was in his room and he spotted her. "Thought you could hide, did you, whore? Just like your fucking mother, a prick tease," he spat at her.

She was up the corner of his room and he cracked the whip at her; it came down across her back and wrapped itself around her, and he pulled her over to him with it. "Come on, bitch, what you going to do now, you can't get away," he said as he put his face in hers. She managed to break free and ran onto the balcony. "Come on, look what Daddy's got for you," he said as he rubbed himself up at the front, and she could see the bulge in his trousers. She was trapped and terrified. He came hurriedly towards her, knowing she had nowhere to run, but as he did so the whip wrapped around his ankles and he stumbled and crashed against the wooden balustrades of the balcony. Because they were old and neglected, they gave way under his weight and he was gone.

Vicky crouched in the corner with her eyes shut tight. Silence closed in around her. She opened her eyes and looked down to the ground through the gap in the balcony and there he was, lying on the ground, motionless. The whip was by her side on the floor. She slowly got up, wincing with pain. She kicked the whip under the bed, not wanting to touch it, and went downstairs and out into the garden where he was. She cautiously went over to him but knew he was dead, as he had blood running from his mouth and his eyes were staring at the sky. She kicked him, and when she realised that he was truly dead she kicked him again and again. "I hate you, you bastard," she sobbed as she kicked. She caught hold of herself, and stopped and walked back into the house. She changed her dress and made herself look as respectable as she could, and phoned for an ambulance. She told them he had fell from the balcony in a drunken stupor and that he was dead. She wasn't lying, and about half an hour later they were there. When they had gone about an hour later, after asking her questions and taking his body away, she collapsed onto the sofa and sobbed. She wasn't crying for him, far from it; she was crying because at last she was free from the beatings and the abuse she had suffered but, most of all , because she was frightened, as she was now on her own.

She made all the arrangements for the funeral, and everyone that knew him came. She wished she could shout out loud and tell everyone what a bastard he really was. The Armstrong's were there, though she hadn't seen them for two years ,as her father had stopped taking her because he couldn't have a hold on her there, and she had missed them all. They had come to visit them a few times but Vicky had been banished to her room, and they had been told she was out. They came over to her and Dolly put her arms around her and she winced because of the pain across her back. She didn't think anyone had seen the pain in her face, but when she looked up she saw Eric looking at her, frowning; she just gave him a shy smile. He was now twenty-five and had grown into a gorgeous dark-haired blue-eyed man. David too had grown up lovely; he was now twenty-three and when they stood side by side they looked rather intimidating, as they were both really tall and broad due to all the rugby they used to play, along with going to the gym. Dolly released her and Tony also gave her a hug, telling her not to worry. She tried to hide her face that time but couldn't, and found that Eric was watching her.

"Do you know that you will be coming to live with us now?" Dolly said, holding her hand.

"No, I didn't, why's that then," Vicky whispered.

"Well, when you were younger, your mom and dad asked us that if anything ever happened to them before you were twenty-one, would we would take care of you, and we agreed because you are like a daughter to us. So that means now you are safe with us until then." Tony told her. Vicky had to sit down. She had always known that this was a special family, full of love and warmth, but had never imagined going to live with them. She felt a sense of relief come over her and started to cry.

"Hey, don't cry, we're not really that bad," Eric said as he sat down next to her, taking her hand.

She looked up at him with tears in her eyes. "Sorry, I know that, it's just that I'm so relieved not to be on my own or have to stay in this house any longer on my own," she said, looking at him.

"You will never be on your own whilst we're here, I promise. Are you okay?" he said, looking at her with concern in his eyes.

"Yes, I'm fine, honest. Thank you. I'll have to go and see to the guests," she said, and with that got up to go, wincing as she moved. She did the rounds with the guests; there weren't that many but they all gave their condolences and wished her well. She just wished she had it in her to shout from the roof tops what a mean, nasty, abusive, vindictive piece of shit her dad really was and they didn't know him at all, so would they all just fuck off and leave her alone. Apart from the Armstrong's, whom she knew and loved.

When all the guests had gone, Dolly and Vicky went up to her room and packed her some clothes and belongings into a bag. "You haven't got many clothes and stuff, have you sweetheart?" Dolly said, looking a bit concerned. Vicky couldn't tell her that her father never used to buy her anything because he was too bloody mean. It had been two years since she had a new dress, and that was for the last time they went to Dolly's house. Nothing she owned fitted her very well; it was just a good job she was on the skinny side of slim. "Never mind, we can soon rectify that, you and me can go shopping if you want, and kit you out with some new fancy clothes," Dolly said as she hugged her.

"Thank you," Vicky whispered.

Dolly saw the look of embarrassment on Vicky's face and said no more, but she was concerned about her as she was so quiet and timid, not like the little girl she remembered growing up, full of life. Mind, when she came to think of it, she hadn't seen her like that, really, for years. They went back downstairs and started clearing all the mess away. Vicky noticed that Eric kept watching her and she was becoming self-conscious.

He came over to her when he saw that she had seen him. "It's okay, I'm not going to pounce on you, it's just that you look like you're in pain. Are you all right?" he asked.

"Yes, I'm fine really, thanks, just got a bit of backache," she lied as she cleared the plates and glasses away. As they left the house when they had cleared away and locked everything up, Vicky felt as if her life was taking a turn at last. She turned and locked the door and, to herself, she said, "Rot in hell, Daddy, you bastard; you will never be able to get to me again." And with that she turned and walked to the car. She sat between Eric and David on the journey back and had never felt so safe in her life. Now she had to get herself in some sort of order and work out what she wanted to do with the rest of her life.

CHAPTER ONE

When they arrived back, they all piled in the house. Eric and David were playing up as usual, joking about with each other. They were really close. Vicky sat and watched them, realising that now they were the closest thing to family she would ever have. "Would it be all right if I went and had a bath?" Vicky asked Dolly as she prepared some supper. She wanted to soothe the welts on her back and wash away the remnants of Daddy dearest for the last time.

"Yes, that's fine love, you don't have to ask, you know where everything is. This is your home now, so treat it as your own, okay?" Dolly said, looking over at her and smiling. Vicky gave her a hug, then went upstairs and started to run herself a bath just as Eric was coming down the stairs.

She looked at him through her lashes and smiled a shy smile. "Are you settling in all right, Vicky?" he asked as he reached the halfway landing on the stairs.

"Yes, fine thanks, I'm just running a bath and I'm going to have a soak. I'm really tired, so I think I will go straight to bed," she said.

"Oh, I thought you might like to come down and have a drink with us all," he said, trying to hide his disappointment. When he saw Vicky that day at the funeral he couldn't believe just how much she had blossomed in the last two years. Yes, admittedly, she had changed and gone quiet and sort of withdrawn, but he knew deep down something was bothering her, and he was worried about her.

"Okay, I will come down for half an hour with you when I have had my bath," she said, looking at him. She had always had a soft spot for Eric and got on well with him, but now she was seeing him in a different light. He was one of those textbook men, as you call them. Tall, dark and handsome, and she was finding it hard not to be attracted to him. But she knew that nothing would ever come of it because no one would ever want her once they had seen the state of her body, with its scars from nearly ten years of whipping and beating off the bastard that called himself her Daddy, especially someone like Eric. She shuddered at the thought of it.

"You okay?" Eric asked, seeing her.

"Yes, fine really, I'm just tired. I will be down in about half an hour, is that okay?" she asked, looking at him. Eric smiled at her, a perfect smile, she thought, wishing for some reason that she could reach up and touch his face. She turned towards the bathroom.

"That's good with me," Eric said, frowning as she went. She undressed in the bathroom, and turned and looked at herself in the mirror. Her small body was covered in scars, with her back being the worst. She had a welt scar that wrapped itself around her, coming from her back round to her stomach, and then loads of others across her back and across the tops of her legs and buttocks. She resembled an A to Z, if you looked too long. Who on earth would ever find her body attractive? Yes, she had a good figure, a little skinny but not too much, but that was about it. She lowered herself into the bath and the last of Daddy's beatings stung as she got into the warm water. She lay there and closed her eyes, relishing the comfort the water gave her.

"Get here, bitch, I'm going to fuck you senseless, you useless little whore," and down came the whip again. Vicky woke with a start, splashing water over the side of the bath. Her breathing was ragged. God, would she ever get away from him? He was giving her nightmares from his grave, haunting her mind. She got out and dried herself carefully, trying not to knock the scabs that were forming on her back. She put on her robe and went downstairs.

***

The four of them were there in the sitting room, and it was so welcoming she felt a lump come to her throat. "Come on, love, come and sit down here by me," Dolly said as she patted the big soft sofa where she was sitting.

Eric watched her cross the room and again noticed her wince as she sat down. She really was lovely, he thought, and he found himself wanting to put his arms round her and hold her tight. They sat and talked about everything, and it was decided that Eric and Tony would sort out some people to go and pack the house up to sell it, with just the personal things being brought here. "Oh yes, I nearly forgot. You remember Sarah, Eric and David's cousin? Well, she has asked if you would like to be bridesmaid at her wedding next month," Dolly said to Vicky.

She didn't know what to say; she had never in her life done anything like that. "Yes, that would be lovely, thank you," she found herself saying.

"Great, I will phone her tomorrow and then she will arrange for some one to come and measure you up for your dress," Dolly said smiling at her. Vicky blanched. Measuring her up. Would that mean she would have to undress? She hoped not.

***

Two days later, Marianne, the girl who was making the dresses, came to see her and measured her up. Luckily, Vicky didn't have to undress. Marianne told her that she would be back in two days for her fitting. Then she did start to worry, but surely she would be able to undress in private. .She would be okay, she thought.

Marianne kept to her word and on Thursday night dropped off Vicky's dress almost finished. "Come on then, love. Let's get you into this," Dolly said as they went into the back dining room.

"I'll be fine, I'll manage," Vicky said, panic rising in her throat. Dolly lay the dress down on the chair and, without Vicky realising, come up behind her and unzipped the back of her dress.

Vicky spun round, her dress falling off one shoulder and revealing the scars across her back. "NO!!" she screamed and fell to the floor on her knees, clutching the front of her dress sobbing, the whole of her back on view.

Dolly was round her in an instance. "Dear god, sweetheart, what has happened to you?" she asked as she put her arms round her. Just then Eric came crashing in, wondering what had happened. He stopped dead when he saw his mom on the floor with Vicky, and saw the scars across her back.

"What the fuck!" he said as he looked. Dolly looked up at him and waved him away. Vicky was sobbing; she turned and looked at Eric and he could see all the pain and suffering in her eyes. He went out as quickly as he went in. He felt sick. How the hell had that happened and nobody had noticed? No wonder she had been wincing when she moved, and was so quiet and withdrawn. She must have been in agony. "Oh Vicky, who has done this to you?" he said to himself. He went into the living room where Tony and David were waiting to hear what was wrong. He told them and they couldn't believe it. "If we know the bastard who's done this I will fucking kill him with my bare hands. I swear I will. Who could hurt her like that, for fuck's sake?" Eric ranted as he paced the room.

Tony looked over at his son. He knew there and then that Eric was falling in love with Vicky. They had always been close; he just hoped that she could feel the same after all this. Half an hour later Dolly came into the room with Vicky, who was looking at the floor, too ashamed to look anyone in the face. She had told Dolly everything; she felt she owed her that. Dolly was pale and in shock.

"Come on, love, sit down," Tony said as he ushered her to a chair.

Eric was over to Vicky and lifted her chin with his finger. "Hey, don't you be frightened to look at us, we're all here for you, remember that," he said and kissed her forehead. They all sat down and Vicky quietly relayed the story she had told Dolly.

Nobody said a word; they couldn't believe it. Suddenly: "Eight fucking years he beat the living crap out of you and you never said anything. Not a fucking whisper off you," Eric ranted. He was seething.

"ERIC, mind what you say," Tony shouted at him with anger. "I can't believe that I classed him as a good mate and yet I never even suspected anything. Why didn't you come to us, sweetheart?" Tony said gently to Vicky.

"I couldn't; he said that if I said anything to anybody it would get worse and believe me, it was bad enough as it was, and I was frightened," she whispered.

Eric went over to her and wrapped his arms gently round her "I'm sorry I shouted. I wasn't shouting at you, I'm just so mad that we never noticed," he said. She started sobbing, great racking sobs, and he just held her there her head against his chest. Dolly and Tony couldn't believe that a friend of theirs could be so malicious to his own daughter.

Vicky's sobbing eased a bit and she stood back a little and looked up at Eric. "Thank you. But I'm sorry, I've wet your shirt," she said, putting her fingers on his chest and wiping the tears off his shirt.

Her fingers felt like heaven against the material on his chest; he found himself wishing that they could stay like this. He clasped her hand against his chest. "It's all right, I'm always here for you, remember that," he said and folded his arms back round her, wishing he could protect her from everything.

***

The next few days went by and Vicky started to feel better about herself. She felt like she had had a ton of weight lifted off her shoulders; now she didn't have a dirty secret any more, and it felt good. She just wished she could get rid of the nightmares that plagued her. Dolly treated her just like a daughter, and took her shopping and did all the motherly things she had missed.

Eric had got some house clearance people into her dad's house and all the personal stuff had been delivered here. Even though Eric now had his own construction company and was busy working every day, he never failed to come and sit with her every night, and David too, sometimes. All three enjoyed each other's company.

The one night David had gone out with Tony and Dolly, Vicky had asked Eric if he would help her sort out all the papers and things of her dad's. They set to, each starting on a box of stuff, and threw away anything that wasn't of importance. Vicky came across a folder with her name on it and when she opened it and read the first page, she had to sit down. "Oh god," she gasped as she sat holding the piece of paper.

Eric was over to her in a shot. "What's wrong?" he asked. She handed him the paper and he read it. "Bloody hell, Vicky."

She was adopted when she was born. "I don't believe it. All those years of him, the bastard, and he's not even my real bloody dad," Vicky said, looking up at Eric "I wonder if that's why he used to say my mother was a whore, and he said the same to me all those years. I never did understand why he said it."

Eric put his arm round her and kissed her temple, comforting her. The paper had her real mother's name on it, but not her real father's. She put it to one side, not being able to take it all in. She would ask Tony and Dolly when they came back. They continued to sort through when Eric found "Daddy dear's" will.

"Do you want to open it?" Vicky said as she sat cross-legged on the floor.

"Are you sure?" Eric said, looking down at her; she nodded and he ripped the envelope open and went and sat on the floor with her. They read it together. Her father had left everything to her, including his accountancy business, the house, the lot, all except a sum of twenty-five thousand pounds to be paid to Dolly and Tony, should she still be under twenty-one when he died. His bank books were in the box too, and they couldn't believe it: there was enough money in there to do Vicky the rest of her life.

"Eight hundred and twenty-six thousand pounds! Jesus, Eric, why did the bastard make me suffer when he had all this?" she asked, looking up at him.

"I can't answer you that, sweetheart," he said as he put his arm round her shoulders. She winced, as she was still sore. "I'm sorry," he said as he moved his arm.

"No, please don't move. I like it, it makes me feel safe when you're around," she said as she put her head on his shoulder. Eric put his arm back round her and smiled, and they sat there for a while, just being content with each other. They continued to sort the remainder of the boxes. Vicky was still on the floor, opening one of the last ones. When she took the lid off it, she screamed and scuttled back across the floor away from the box.

"Vicky, whatever's wrong," Eric said as he rushed over to her and held her. She was visibly shaking, suddenly a wreck. He let her go and went over to the box and even he blanched: there inside was the leather whip and the riding crop that had beaten her for so long. He did no more than get the box and go and throw it outside. "It's okay, sweetheart," he said when he came back and put his arms round her again and held her tight, being careful of her sores. "Oh Vicky, why have you had to suffer like this? You are the most wonderful, kindest, sexiest woman I have ever known. I think I love you," he said as he kissed her hair.

She pulled away from him and looked up at him. "How can you love me when I'm scarred like I am and you've seen me, and I'm sometimes not in a sound state of mind either," she whispered.

"I love you because you're you and in time you will be better. I know you will," he said as he lowered his head and their lips met for the first time in a kiss that said it all. There was hunger and passion in that first kiss from both of them. As they parted they looked at each other. "Jesus, Vicky. Now I know I love you, more than anything."

"I love you too. I think I always have, deep down."

They sat on the floor and he just held her, wanting to protect her from everything and everybody. It was the beginning of a strong passionate protective love that would grow even stronger between them.

***

Later that evening when everyone was home, they told them all about their findings and decided to tell them about themselves too. Tony and Dolly were just as shocked as Vicky to find out that she was adopted. They sat and talked about things for a while, and Dolly and Tony could see what Eric and Vicky were like with each other. It was as if they had been together all their lives, understood each other and had a special bond that only they knew. They were inseparable. Suddenly, Dolly couldn't keep it in any longer. "Well, we couldn't wish for a better daughter-in-law than you, sweetheart," Dolly said, winking at Vicky.

"Bloody hell, Mom, give us a chance" Eric said, nearly choking on his drink. They all burst out laughing.

"Well, it's not like you have got to get to know each other, is it, son?" Tony added, laughing still.

Even Vicky was laughing, something she hadn't done for a while. "You know, you look gorgeous when you laugh," Eric said as he put his arms round her.

"I love you," she whispered in his ear, and his arms tightened round her protectively.

***

The next few weeks were spent sorting out "Daddy dearest's" things. Eric had done most of it for her as she couldn't stand to have anything to do with it, and he understood this and wanted to protect her from it. She was still having nightmares, waking up screaming, and Dolly would stay with her in her room. Even though Eric wished it was him instead, he knew she was safe with his mom. Their love for each other blossomed, and they became really close.

"I'm thinking of buying a house," he told them all one day when he came in from work. Vicky just looked at him. "Don't worry, sweetheart, I want you to see it first," he said as he came over and kissed her. "Come on, we're going for a drive," he said and took her hand, winking at his dad. They were in the car and on their way in minutes.

"Where are we going?" Vicky asked quietly.

Eric did no more than pull over into a lay-by, and gently pulled her into his arms and kissed her. "I love you, Vicky Foster, and I want to marry you and make you happy. I know it's early days for us yet but I don't think that we will ever have a problem. Will you make me the happiest man alive and marry me?" he said and kissed her gently on her lips.

Vicky looked up into his eyes. "Yes I will, and you already make me happy, and I love you more than anything," she whispered as she snaked her hands up round his neck into his hair and kissed him longingly.

"Jesus, Vicky, the things you do to me." She smiled up at him and they kissed with a passion. They pulled back out and carried on their journey only to turn into a little village a few minutes later. They pulled onto an arched driveway and there stood the most gorgeous house Vicky had ever seen.

"Well, this is it. I hope you like it and it's only a stones throw from mom and dad. What's your first impression?"

"It's gorgeous."

"Well, I hope you think the same about the inside. It needs a bit of love, but I know you will soon sort that out. Come on, let's have a look." They got out of the car and went up the three steps to the door. He opened it and turned to look at her, smiling. "What's going on in that pretty little head of yours, Miss Foster?" he asked as he gazed down at her.

"Nothing, I'm just amazed by this house. It's lovely, Eric, it really is," and she reached up to him and kissed him.

He circled his arms round her. "This is how I love to see you, sweetheart, happy and smiling. Let me take all your demons away from you and protect you," he said as he kissed her.

"Oh, Eric, I think you have already started to do that, because what you do to me helps me forget. I know it will probably never go away altogether, but when I'm with you I feel safe and loved."

"That's how I want you to feel, because I do love you very much. Come on, let's look round." He held her hand and they took a tour of the house.

* * *

After two weeks of sorting out builders, decorators, plumbers and electricians, Vicky had organised for them all to meet at the house, and the jobs to do were sorted and work started. "How's things going down there, Vicky?" David asked her one morning at breakfast.

"It's coming along fine at the moment, just waiting for materials to arrive and then Josh the decorator can get started on the master bedroom. He has finished the three guest rooms and the bathrooms and they are looking fabulous, even though I say it myself," she replied, trying not to sound too boastful because she was really pleased with how things were turning out.

"Well, we all know that you will do yourself and big brother proud. He is always singing your praises so I think he knows you will, too. " He got up from the table. "Anyway, I had better be off, else I will be late. Bye. See you later." He kissed his mom and her as he left the kitchen.

"Well, you have made Eric really happy, young lady. And we couldn't be happier for you both. And, as David just said, he can't stop talking about what you are doing and that he can't wait to see the house finished, but there, again, none of us can wait to see it. We all know that you will do a brilliant job," Dolly said as she cleared away the breakfast things. Then she came round the table and gave Vicky a great big hug.

One month later, everyone was seated around the table at home having one of Dolly's scrumptious roast dinners. "How's everything going now, Vicky?" Tony asked her as he filled his mouth with another roast potato.

"Well, apart from the hiccup we had with the light switches and the main bathroom shower fittings, all is going to plan. But I have put a hold on the main bathroom for now because I have had another idea for it, so it's going to be one of the last things done."

"What's the idea you have had then, sweetheart? I thought that it was all going to plan perfectly," Eric said as he helped himself to more veg.

"Oh, it is, but I have had an idea for the bathroom but I want to wait to put it to plan and no, I'm not going to tell you what it is so don't ask," she said, smiling at him.

"Okay, I won't, I've been told," he said as he gave her a wink, and Vicky's heart leapt. They had grown so close the last couple of months, and Vicky couldn't have been happier. "I think that you and me should have a drive down there tomorrow, being as it's Sunday, and you can show me what's happening, then we can go and have lunch in that little pub, the Golden Thistle, if you would like to," Eric said as he looked across the table at her.

"That would be lovely, but I thought you didn't want to see it until it was finished," she said.

"Well, I think it is time that I put my plan into action, the plan I have had from the beginning and tomorrow seems like the ideal time, and no I'm not going to tell you either, so don't ask me," he said as he gave her another wink across the table, smiling at her.

The following morning Eric was down to breakfast early and his mom just kept smiling at him. "What's got into you?" he asked as she poured him a cup of tea.

"Nothing, son, I'm just happy for you, that's all, can't a mother be happy for her son without being questioned over it?" she said, and promptly gave him a great big hug.

"Women," he said. "They cease to amaze me."

Vicky came down about ten minutes later, and Eric came over and kissed her. "Morning, sweetheart, you okay?" he asked, as he knew she had had another nightmare last night, waking up screaming.

"Yes, I am now, thanks."

Half an hour later Eric was driving them both to Little Haven with a smile on his face that made him look like a boy again. They turned into the village and in no time were pulling up outside their house. "Come on, let's get inside," he said as he opened the door. "I can't wait to see what you've done to the place and I have got something I want to do as well."

They walked into the hall and Eric stood stock still. "My god, Vicky, what have you done!" he said as he looked around.

"Oh no, you don't like it do you? I thought that you would love it like this, it seems so homely and cosy," Vicky said, dispirited.

Eric turned around with a look in his eyes that she didn't recognise. "I love it, Vicky, it's fantastic, you've transformed the place," he said as he looked down at her, smiling.

"Thank heavens for that, I thought I'd got it all wrong for you. I really want you to love it like I do, Eric. Come on, let me show you the rest" and at that she walked into the kitchen with Eric close behind.

"You've done a fantastic job. I'm really proud of you," he said as he turned and looked at her. Yet, again, he had that look in his eyes she didn't recognise. He couldn't get over just how she had transformed the whole of the house. "It's wonderful, Vicky," he said as they sat down with a glass of wine from the bottle Eric had brought with them. After that, they went upstairs and she showed him round all the rooms, leaving the room that was to be theirs till last. As they entered, she took his hand.

"Wow, this is fantastic, I love the furniture," he said, eyeing up the bed. He turned to her and took her in his arms. "I want you, Vic.

I love you so much, but at this moment I want to show you just how much," he said, looking down at her.

"I want you too, but I've never...."

He put his finger to her lips to stop her. "I know," he whispered, and kissed her gently. They kissed as they moved over to the bed and Eric gently started to undo her blouse. He felt her tense up. "Don't worry, sweetheart, I know your scars are there and they don't bother me because I love you, and I want to kiss them for you to show you they don't bother me."

She put her arms round his neck and he gently lowered her onto the bed. His tongue found hers as they kissed, and the kisses became harder. He started to work his way down her neck and onto her stomach with feather-light kisses. She felt him kiss all the way across the scar on her stomach. She reached down and put her hands in his hair; he carried on kissing her, working his way back up. "Oh Jesus, Vicky, I love you," he gasped, and he undid her skirt and pulled it down her legs.

She could feel the hardness of him against her, and she knew she wanted him more than anything. She undid his trousers and he pulled them and his boxers down, releasing himself onto her. He slid on top of her and gently eased himself into her. "Oh Jesus," she gasped.

"You okay?" he whispered as he leaned up on his elbows and looked down at her, kissing her.

"Perfect," she whispered back. Their eyes met and the passion rose within the two of them. Their rhythm came together as she wrapped her legs around his waist and he brought her to a height she had never known before, a magical dizzy height and she loved it. He too reached his height, releasing himself into her and calling out her name as he did. They collapsed together, holding one another tight as their breathing steadied.

He rolled onto his side, pulling her with him, and they lay there entwined together. "You okay, sweetheart?" he said as he kissed her cheek.

She turned and looked up at him, smiling. "I don't think I have ever been better," she said, and she put her head on his chest and lay there feeling totally and utterly safe and loved until they fell to sleep.

"No, Daddy, no more, it hurts," she cried.

Eric was awake in seconds, pulling her to him "It's okay, sweetheart, I'm here. It's just a dream." And he lay cradling her in his arms, trying to suppress her shaking.

"I'm sorry," she whispered after a few minutes.

"Hey, you don't have to be sorry for anything," he said, tilting her head up to him with his fingers and kissing her. He held her tight, feeling like he could cry for her.

A couple of hours later they were in the Golden Thistle, having talked about everything and kissed so many times that neither of them could count. "Shall we eat now, or just have a drink and go home?" Eric asked as he looked across the table at her and squeezed her hand.

"I'm not hungry now really, only for you. I just want to go on loving you. I can't believe this is real. I love you so much, Eric," she said.

"And I love you more than anything," he said, smiling and feeling as if his heart would burst.

With that, they left the Golden Thistle after one drink and started the drive home. Just before they reached home, Eric pulled over. "Why have we stopped?" Vicky asked, looking puzzled.

"Just so that I can do this," Eric said huskily as he reached over to her and pulled her to him, kissing her so tenderly yet hungrily that Vicky couldn't get her breath. "Shall we make a date for the wedding?" he said as he kissed her again.

"Yes, I think we should, we have wasted enough time," she said as she returned his kiss. They arrived home and entered into the kitchen, where Dolly and Tony were having a cup of tea.

"Well, you two look rather sheepish; what have you been up to?" Tony said as they sat down.

Eric looked at Vicky and smiled. "We're going to make a date for the wedding," Eric finally said.

"Well, about bloody time, too. Jesus! Me and your mother were beginning to think that neither of you would ever come to your senses, and you were going to take forever." Tony laughed as he hugged Dolly, and she was wiping her eyes with her apron.

"Well, lad, it was as plain as the nose on your face that you two love each other like anything. It just took you both ages to realise that you need to be married; we've known it for ages," Dolly sniffed. "Oh, I am so happy for you both, we both are. Wait till your brother knows; even he will breathe a sigh of relief," she said.

That night over tea, the date was set for a June wedding in just three weeks' time, with Sarah being her maid of honour.

CHAPTER TWO

The wedding took place on June 12, 1985 at Little Haven parish church. The weather was fine and sunny, and Sarah looked wonderful in her bridesmaid dress, just as Vicky did at her wedding. David was Eric's best man. The day was perfect. The reception was held in the Golden Thistle and everyone from workplaces and around came. "Are you happy, Mrs Armstrong?" Eric whispered in Vicky's ear as they danced.

"Blissfully," she sighed as she rested her head on his shoulder.

"You've looked gorgeous all day. Do you know that?" he said.

"You've looked rather fetching yourself," she smiled up at him.

"You're safe with me now, sweetheart; nobody will ever hurt you again," he said, and he rested his cheek on her head and they danced. With the reception coming to an end, people were starting to leave. All the family were staying at the hotel just in the next village. Only Eric and Vicky were going to their house, to spend their first night together in their newly decorated home. Everything was finished now, even the main bathroom (to Vicky's delight). They would go on their honeymoon to New York Monday morning.

Everyone said their good-nights and Eric and Vicky walked down to their house. Once there Eric did no more than scoop her up in his strong arms and carried her over the threshold. With the door closed behind them they stood and kissed for what seemed like an eternity. Eric then picked her up again and carried her up the stairs and into the main bedroom. "Vicky, I love you so much," he said as he undid the buttons down the back of her dress. "I want you more than anything at this moment." With that, her dress slipped down and fell at her feet. He bent and kissed her scarred back, working his way round to her mouth.

By now Vicky was undoing Eric's shirt and the feeling of electricity between them was unbelievable. They fell onto the bed with Eric kissing her breasts and sucking her nipples so softly she didn't know if she would be able to control herself. They carried on until their height of passion could no longer contain itself. Eric entered her so gently and passionately she thought that her heart would burst with love for this man she had loved for so long. Eric couldn't believe that he could love anyone with so much passion as he did with Vicky that night. It was a chapter of love that was just beginning in their lives.

***

Christmas that year would be celebrated in style. They had been married six wonderful months and the whole family was coming for Christmas. Even David and his new fiancée Cora were coming to stay. Tony and Dolly were the first ones to arrive, Dolly bringing the biggest turkey you have ever seen, Tony with three bottles of whisky. "Hello son, how are you doing?" he said as Eric opened the door. "No need to ask, really; I can see by the look of you that you are contented and happy," he continued.

"Hello Dad, and yes I am, thanks, couldn't wish for anything more." Within an hour everyone was there; it was Christmas Eve and the drinks were flowing. Eric went up behind Vicky in the kitchen and put his arms around her waist. "How's my girl doing? Do you want any help?"

"I'm fine, thanks, sweetheart, but would cope better if you didn't keep teasing me like that. You know what it does to me," she said as she turned around and kissed him.

"I know; that's why I do it. Just you wait till later," he teased, and with that he kissed the tip of her nose, winked at her and made a hasty retreat into the living room with Vicky throwing the tea towel at him, smiling. It was the best Christmas Vicky had ever known.

***

Christmas and New Year were over, and everyone had gone home and back to work. Eric now had an office closer to home and Vicky had her accounts business close by. Every lunchtime they would meet back at home and usually didn't get any lunch because they would end up making love wherever they landed. They just couldn't get enough of each other. The only problem was, Vicky still had her nightmares and Eric would cradle her in his arms every time.

Early in March Vicky started to feel ill. She didn't know why, and didn't say anything to Eric. She made an appointment at the doctor's and couldn't believe it when he told her that she was about two months pregnant. She raced home and nearly fell through the front door. "Eric, Eric, where are you, sweetheart?" she shouted.

Eric came crashing out of the study. "What's up, what's wrong?" he asked when he saw the look on her face.

"I'm pregnant," she blurted out with sheer joy.

"Oh Jesus, I don't believe it," Eric said as he scooped her up and swung her round, kissing every part of her neck and face that he could. Later that evening when it had sunk in to both of them that it was real, Eric said to her, "Why didn't you tell me that you were feeling ill?"

"I didn't think it would be anything serious, I just kept feeling queasy," she said as she curled up against him on the settee.

"I love you beyond reason, Vicky; please tell me if you're not feeling right and it will stop me worrying so much," he said as he kissed her.

"I'm sorry, sweetheart, I promise in future I will, but the same goes for you too, okay?" she said as she returned his kiss and curled back up against him, hugging him.

The family was elated. Dolly was beside herself with joy. Her first grandchild! Tony took Eric and David out to celebrate, and Vicky stayed in with Dolly and had a quiet girlie's night in.

***

Suddenly, one night in May, Vicky started getting really bad pains in her stomach. "Eric," she whispered as she turned to him, shaking him. Eric woke to find Vicky doubled up in agony. "Oh God, please no," he said as he picked up the phone to ring for an ambulance. Within half an hour Vicky was in intensive care. She had lost the baby, and so much blood she had to have a transfusion. Eric was beside himself. He rang his mom and dad and told them, and half an hour later they were there with David.

"Any more news yet, son?" Tony said as they walked in.

"Nothing yet, just that she is in an induced coma so her body can recoup itself. Oh God, Mom, I couldn't bear to lose her as well, not now, not ever," Eric said as his mother hugged him. The nurse came and told Eric he could go into his wife, but not to disturb her.

"We'll let you in on your own first, son," Tony said as he patted Eric's shoulder.

"Thanks, Dad." Eric entered the room and all he could see was his sweet and precious wife lying with tubes and drips all over her. He sat down at the side of the bed and took Vicky's hand. "Come on, sweetheart, pull through for me. I couldn't cope without you now. You are my world. I love you more than anything," he whispered as tears began to roll down his face. He sat there until he had pulled himself together a bit, then went out and called in the others.

Dolly couldn't cope and had to go back out. Tony put his arm round his sons shoulder and hugged him. "She'll pull through son because she knows she has you here" was all he could say. With that he left the room and went to take Dolly home. Eric spent the next three days and nights next to Vicky.

The nurse had told him they were going to slowly bring her out of the coma, so all he could do was wait. The following day Eric was sitting with his head on the bed holding Vicky's hand. Suddenly, her fingers folded around his. Eric looked up to see that she was awake. He stood up and gently kissed her lips. "Hello, sweetheart."

Vicky looked up at him and slowly gave him a watery smile.

"I'm just going to get the nurse, okay?" he said as he kissed her again. After the nurse and doctor had done all the checks they had to, they left the room.

"I'm sorry," Vicky suddenly said.

"Sorry for what, sweetheart? You haven't done anything wrong," Eric said, looking at her.

"I've lost our baby," she whispered.

"Vicky, sweetheart, you haven't done anything. Unfortunately, it's Mother Nature, and yes, I'm devastated too. But I still have you, which is something I thought I had lost as well. And you have me right by your side for whatever and whenever you want, you know that."

Eric was talking so softly Vicky's heart went out to him. "Hold me, Eric. I need to feel your arms around me," she said, looking up at him. He bent over her and scooped her up in his arms. And there they remained until visiting ended, holding each other and crying together.

A week later Vicky was discharged from hospital and Eric took her straight to his mom and dad's. "We're going to stay here for a bit until you're on your feet properly. I don't want you overdoing anything; I want my happy brave Vicky back by my side. Is that okay with you?" Eric said to Vicky as they pulled up outside.

"That's fine with me, I can cope with your mom's cooking and fussing any day of the week," she said, turning to him and kissing his cheek. He winked at her and got out the car and went into the house.

"Hello, princess," Tony said as they walked into the kitchen. "How are you feeling today? Here, come and sit down by me," he said, patting the big comfy sofa they had in the kitchen.

"I'm feeling a lot better now, thanks, Tony, and I'm not crying quite so much, but I think a lot of that is down to Eric because he has been perfect," she said as she looked lovingly up at her husband.

"Flattery will get you everywhere, you know," he said as he bent and kissed the top of her head. That night in bed Eric cradled her in his arms and they quietly wept together for the loss of the baby they would have both loved.

***

Seven weeks went by and Vicky regained her strength and sanity again even though the nightmares still came. Eric had watched his wife slowly return to something like her old self. "Shall we think of going home, Eric?" Vicky said to him one morning.

"Do you think that you are ready, sweetheart?" he replied as he got ready for work.

"Well, yes, I am, simply because I can't wait to have you to myself again," she said as she lay on the bed smiling up at him.

"Now now, Mrs Armstrong, you just behave yourself, else I just might have to get back into bed with you and teach you how," he said as he came over to her and sat on the bed.

"Now that sounds like a perfect idea," she whispered as she pulled him towards her. Within minutes they were making love for the first time in weeks, and every passionate emotion came pouring out of both of them.

Eric was so gentle with her; he was all she would ever want, her own gentle giant. He kissed her all over, relishing her body. "I love you, Vicky Armstrong. Don't you ever forget that," he said as he entered her again, making her groan with desire for him and pull him to her. They reached their heights and collapsed in a tangled mass together on the bed, catching their breath as they kissed.

***

They returned home the following weekend and everything returned to as normal as it could be. Vicky returned to her office and took the reins back from her manager Stuart. "I would like to thank you, Stuart, for taking good care of things whilst I have been away, and I will look after you in your pay packet, don't worry," she said as she began to sort through some of the paperwork.

"It's been a pleasure, Vicky. I must say one other thing, though, and that is that it is good to have you back and looking well again. Coffee?" he asked as he went to put the kettle on in the back.

"Yes, please, that would be lovely."

***

Their second anniversary passed, and things couldn't be any better between them. They loved each other beyond belief and couldn't get enough of each other even though the nightmares still plagued Vicky, and Eric would just hold her tight until she stopped shaking. It was now November and the shops were filling up for Christmas. "Mom has asked if we would like to go there for Christmas this year, sweetheart, what do you say to it?" Eric said one evening when they were laying curled up on the sofa.

"Mm, does that mean I have got to share you with everyone again?" she smiled up at him.

"You are one bad tease, do you know that?" he said as he kissed her nose.

"Yes, I know I am, but you love it really," she said as she climbed on top of him.

"Yes, but not as much as I love you," he said as he pulled her to him and started to undo her blouse. Within minutes they were caressing each other with passion and lust. "Jesus, Vicky, I want you so bad it hurts," Eric whispered in her ear as he kissed her neck.

"Take me with all you have, sweetheart, I'm yours to take," she gasped as he sucked her nipples and caressed her breasts and kissed every part of her body. She undid his trousers and slipped her hand inside, making him need her more.

"Bloody hell, Vicky, do you know what you do to me?" he groaned as he rolled off the settee, gently pulling her down onto him and kissing her. They didn't make love that night; they had raw erotic sex on the living room floor, playing with each other, teasing and tempting . . . it was wonderful.

***

Christmas was upon them and they prepared to go to Mom and Dad's on Christmas Eve night. "Is Cora coming with David this year?" Vicky asked as she got dressed.

"Yes she is, and I think they are going to tell us the wedding date at long last," Eric said as he looked at her in the mirror, smiling at her with a look in his eyes she knew only too well.

"Oh no, not now, Eric Armstrong; I've just put my dress on," she laughed as she got up and ran around the other side of the bed.

"Come here, you tease," he laughed back and caught her by the arm, and they landed on the bed laughing together. Within minutes again they were making love with a passion and yet, again, they couldn't get enough of each other. Eric kissed her all up her spine, making her tingle all over; she didn't need to be embarrassed by her many scars with him, as he always kissed them for her, making her feel wonderful. He always loved her passionately, sometimes with desire, sometimes with lust, but every time was different and she loved him for it. He protected her from everything, even herself. An hour or so later they were getting into the car to drive to Mom and Dad's.

"Mom will think we're not coming. I told her we would be there for eight," Eric said as he pulled off the driveway.

"Well, whose fault is that then?" Vicky said as she leaned over and kissed his cheek, smiling at him.

He turned and looked at her and smiled back. "But it was worth it, wasn't it?" he said, raising his eyebrow as he winked at her.

"Every second," she said, giving him a cheeky smile. They arrived only forty minutes late and no one said anything.

"How is my young lady tonight?" Tony asked as they all sat in the living room with a drink.

"I'm good, thank you, Tony, couldn't be better, but then again I've got the best person in the world looking after me, haven't I?" Vicky said as she looked at Eric.

"Well, he knows he'd have me to answer to if he didn't," he laughed. David and Cora told them all that they had set a date for their wedding. It would be next July. Everyone congratulated them. They had a few more drinks and chatted. Eric was telling David about a contract he was going after at work, worth a lot of money, and David was all for it.

That night, as Vicky and Eric were getting ready for bed, Vicky turned to him. "Eric, do you think we should try for another baby yet?" she said quietly.

Eric looked at her with a sad smile and said, "If you feel you're up to it, sweetheart, then that's no problem with me." He walked over to her and took her in his arms and they stood holding each other for a few minutes. Then Eric looked down at her, cupped her chin with his finger, lifted her head and kissed her with the soft gentle kisses she was so used to having off this wonderful loving man, her gentle giant. "Do you want to start trying now?" he said, smiling down at her with a mischievous look in his eyes.

"Eric Armstrong, you are a husband in a million, do you know that? And I love you so much." She looked up at him and started unbuttoning his shirt.

"Well," he said as he looked down at what she was doing, "I'll take that as a yes, shall I, because you know what you do to me when you start undressing me, I can't control myself."

"I don't want you to control yourself. I want you to have your wicked way with me and leave me wanting more of you," she said as she started kissing his chest and working her way down, reaching and undoing his trousers and releasing the beast from within, taking him in her hand and running her tongue over him, kissing him.

"God, Vicky, you're a wicked tease to me," he groaned as he pulled her back up to him. With that, they finished undressing each other and fell onto the bed and made love continuously for the next few hours, loving every moment of each other. The following morning Eric woke to find Vicky kissing, licking and biting him gently down his back. It was so tantalisingly good feeling her tongue on him. He turned to her and pulled her to him, and before he knew it she straddled him, and as he grabbed her hips, he lifted her and entered her and they were making love yet again, raking at each others' bodies.

"Vicky Armstrong, you are a bad influence on me!" he said as they both lay there afterwards.

"Well, I've had a good teacher" she said as he stroked her back and they both burst out laughing.

"I love hearing you laugh; it sounds good," he said as he kissed her and let his hands wander back down her body.

***

Christmas Day was great; everybody enjoyed themselves and had their fill of food and drink. The next few days passed and everything was perfect except that Vicky had another two nightmares, but Eric was there for her as usual, holding her tight next to him till she calmed. Another New Year's Eve came and went, with everyone enjoying themselves as usual. Everyone started leaving New Year's Day afternoon, and things returned back to as normal as they could be.

That night Eric asked Vicky if she had given any more thought about finding her real mom and dad, as it had been nearly three years since "he" had died. She said she hadn't, so Eric left it at that.

February arrived and Eric was run off his feet at work because he had clinched the deal he and David were after on a new build site and was busy sorting plans and builders and et cetera. Vicky of course took control of the finances, seeing as she was the company accountant and a director too. One Wednesday evening as Vicky was preparing the tea at home, Eric walked in with a face that said the cat had got the cream.

"Come on then, how did it go, don't keep me hanging on," Vicky said as she kissed his cheek.

Suddenly, he scooped her up in his arms and swung her around. "The deal's ours and, to top it all, Vance wants it all signed by the end of June." They had known Vance for years; he was retirement age now, another friend of Tony's, but he put any work he could Eric's way because he knew he wouldn't be let down so, that meant two major building deals in one month. "I definitely feel the need to celebrate. Come on, we're going out," he said as he put her back down, kissing her as he did so.

"Not so fast, mister," Vicky said, smiling up at him. "I've got something to say first."

"Sorry, sweetheart, I'm just so happy and excited that everyone's hard work has paid off," he said.

"Well, be prepared to get even happier then," she said as she looked up into his deep blue eyes. "I'm pregnant."

You could have knocked Eric down with a feather. The look on his face went from a smile to a tremendous Cheshire cat grin. "Oh Vicky, just when I thought my day couldn't get any better, you come up trumps. No wonder I love you as much as I do," and at that, he put his strong arms around her, hugged her like there was no tomorrow and kissed her face all over. As he pulled away from her, he stood back. "Is everything okay with it, you know, with last time and all?" he said, looking worried.

"The doctor has told me just to take the next two months relatively easy and I should be okay, but he can't promise anything," she said. "And, hopefully, we will have a Christmas baby," and she put her arms back around Eric and they just stood and held each other.

* * *

July 1988 came, and David and Cora were married. Vicky was maid of honour. She wore a wine-coloured bridesmaid dress and looked stunning apart from the fact that she now had a small bump, being four months pregnant. Later that evening, when the reception was in full swing, Eric came up behind Vicky and put his arms around her. "Can I have the next dance with my beautiful stunning wife" he whispered in her ear.

Vicky turned in his arms, put her arms around his neck and kissed him tenderly on his lips. "You may, kind sir, as long as you promise to be gentle with me later when I take you to bed with me," she teased.

"Oh, you can guarantee that, believe me, Mrs Armstrong, I promise," he teased back as they danced. That night in bed, Vicky's gentle giant lived up to the name she had for him. He was as gentle with her as ever, and the love they made was all both of them needed. Everything was working out better than either of them could have dreamt. Both businesses were doing well. Eric now had a manual hold on all the builders and labourers. He was on site from early morning until late afternoon, and he would always come home dusty and dirty or completely shattered. But he didn't mind one bit, as this was their future.

"Where has my clean-looking, alert husband gone to?" Vicky asked as she smiled at him one evening whilst she prepared dinner.

Eric did no more than get up, go around to her, cup her face between his hands and gently kiss her lips. "I'm still here, sweetheart, have I been neglecting you lately? I'm sorry if I have," he said as he looked at her.

"No, you haven't neglected me at all, quite the opposite actually, I'm just worried that you're overworking yourself. I don't want you tiring yourself out, do I?" she said.

Eric looked down at her, then put his hands on the small lump that was now her stomach. "I won't, don't worry, I'm going to need plenty of energy for this little fellow," he said as he gently rubbed her stomach.

"Oh Eric, I love you so much, I can't help but worry about you, it's natural." She smiled up at him. With that, she kissed him and held him tight for a few minutes.

CHAPTER THREE

The beginning of August came, and everyone was flat out trying to keep to the planned schedule. Eric was helping out with felting the roofs on the porches of one of the houses. He had just got to the bottom of the ladder when there was a sudden crash, men shouting and a lot of commotion. Eric looked up, and that was the last thing he remembered. There had been a terrible accident.

The door of Vicky's office came crashing open; she looked up from where she was and saw Tony and David standing there deathly white. "Hello, you two, what's wrong?" she asked worriedly.

Tony came over to her and put his arms around her. "Vicky, there's been an accident on the site; I'm afraid Eric's on his way to hospital and...."

"Oh God, no, not Eric, what's happened? Where is he?" she said.

"Vicky, Vicky," David said as calmly as he could, putting his arms round her. "Come on, we're going to the hospital, then we will know what's going on, but you have got to take it easy because of the baby, you need to stay as calm as you possibly can."

They drove to the hospital in record time; luckily it wasn't too far. "I've come to see my husband Eric Armstrong; he was brought in not long ago," Vicky said as calmly as she could to the nurse on the desk.

"He has been taken to theatre and at the moment, Mrs Armstrong, they are operating on him," she told them.

"What's happened to him?" Tony asked, because he could see Vicky just wasn't dealing with it at all and he was beginning to worry about her.

"The doctor will come and see you in a minute. I will tell him you're here; please take a seat." the nurse said, pointing to the chairs opposite.

Whilst they were waiting, Dolly arrived. "What's happening?" Dolly asked Tony quietly.

"We're waiting for the doctor to come and see us, but I don't think Vicky should stressing like this; I'm worried about the baby," he whispered to her.

Dolly went and sat by Vicky, and put her arm around her shoulders. "Come on, love, he'll be okay. He's as strong as an ox, remember," she said.

Just then the doctor came. "Mrs Armstrong?" he asked as he looked around.

"That's me," Vicky said quietly. "What's happening to my husband, Doctor? How is he?" she asked.

"Well, he has sustained a head injury and burns to his face," the doctor said.

"Oh no! Is he going to be all right?" Vicky asked. As she sat back down, her legs felt like jelly.

"Hopefully, we have caught everything in time," he said. "The operation is to stop the bleeding from the deep gash he sustained from his left temple to his upper lip, and to give us a chance to clean up the burn he has to his face underneath this cut, and to access his brain movements to make sure there's no damage," the doctor told them.

"When will I be able to see him?" Vicky asked quietly.

"In the morning, as he will be in surgery for another hour, then he will go into a side ward where we will monitor him through the night," the doctor said.

"Thank you, Doctor," Tony said. At that, the doctor turned and left, and Vicky sat motionless on the seat. "Come on, sweetheart," Tony said to Vicky as he helped her up. "We can go back to ours, and then I will bring you back later because I know you won't wait until morning, and I would rather be here with you than worrying at home."

"Thank you," was all Vicky could muster.

On the way home, Dolly was getting more and more worried about Vicky. The colour had gone completely from her face, and she was really quiet. "Mom, do you want me to stay tonight?" David asked, as he could see what his mother was seeing.

"That would be great, David. Thank you, because I wouldn't be able to get to the hospital if you didn't. Dad is already there with Vicky," she said sadly.

"That's okay, I'll just phone Cora and let her know when we get back," he said. Tony and Vicky went back to the hospital two hours later. They were shown into the side ward where Eric was and told everything had gone well, and it was just a matter of waiting to see when he came around.

Vicky went over to the bed and took his hand. "Oh, sweetheart, please be okay. I love you and I'm waiting here for you," she whispered to him, and the tears began to roll down her cheeks.

"Come on, Vicky," Tony said as he came over to her. "You won't be any good to him if you're worn out, will you?" he said as he put his arm around her.

"But I need to stay, Tony. I want to be here when he comes round," she said, looking down at Eric's bandaged face. Just as she had got out her last words, she collapsed on the floor. Tony screamed for the nurse. Two nurses came rushing in and took hold of the situation.

It was Tony who noticed the blood underneath Vicky's legs. "She's bleeding," he yelled at the nurses, as they noticed at the same time. The nurses rushed about, a trolley bed was brought in by the orderly and a doctor arrived within seconds.

"Please, God, don't let them lose this baby," Tony said to himself quietly. Twenty minutes later Tony was on the phone to all at home. Dolly answered. "It's only me, love, I'm afraid I've got some more bad news for you and you will have to come to the hospital, Vicky has collapsed and she has lost the baby. She is in a critical condition, she's lost so much blood, please, Dolly, get here asap," Tony cried down the phone.

"Oh no, not again," Dolly cried also. "We're on our way," she said, and was gone. At the hospital, Tony, Dolly and David all waited for any news on either Eric or Vicky. "I can't believe this has happened today," Dolly sobbed as she was comforted by David. "Neither of them would hurt anyone, and this has to happen to them," she said.

"You do realise, Dad, that when Eric comes round he is going to ask where Vicky is. What are we going to say to him?" David said as he sat holding his mom's hand.

"Lord only knows, son, but we certainly can't tell him what's happened, because it might set him back again," Tony replied sadly.

Five hours later, Eric had come round and, even though he was still groggy, in pain and very sore, he knew something was wrong. "Where's Vicky?" he croaked, as his throat was very sore.

Tony looked over at Dolly. "She's having a rest, son, because she's worn out," he lied. He hated lying to him but knew he would try to get up to go to her if he told him the truth.

"Is she okay, though," he said as he looked around the room.

"Yes, she's just very tired; she'll be in to you soon, don't worry," Tony lied again. "What happened at work son?" Tony asked, trying to get Eric's mind off Vicky.

"I was helping up on the porch roofs, all I remember is that I was nearly at the bottom of the ladder, I heard an almighty crash and loads of shouting, I looked up and all I remember then is that something hit me on the side of the head, now I know it was the tar bucket, it spliced my face and scalded me with tar," he said, trying to think. "I know I'm going to look hideous when these bandages come off, I just hope Vicky will still want me and love me when I look like a freak. I couldn't stand the thought of losing her." he whispered.

Meanwhile David sat in another room down the hospital corridor, with Vicky. She was sedated to keep her still, to stem the bleeding from her womb. She had lost the baby, and had also lost an awful lot of blood and had to have another transfusion. The doctor said it was probably caused by severe stress and panic caused by Eric's accident, added to the fact that she hadn't got a very strong womb due to bruising and damage from when she was younger.

Dolly stayed the night by Vicky's bedside. There hadn't been any improvement in her condition through the night, and they didn't know what to do. Tony and David came back to the hospital after breakfast, and they sat and discussed what they should say to Eric when they went in to see him. At one o'clock they all went in to see Eric. The nurses knew they were going to tell him about Vicky, and were prepared to take him down there in a wheelchair if necessary. "Hello, son" Dolly said as they walked in. "How are you feeling today?"

"Very sore and have a thumping headache, but the doctor said I will have it for a few days yet so I have got to put up with it for now. Where's Vicky again?" he asked, looking round.

"Eric, we've got something to tell you and don't be angry with us for not telling you before, okay?" Tony said as he prepared himself for the worst.

Eric's heart sank and the lump in his throat felt like it was going to choke him. "I know," he said. "She can't stand the thought of being with me now I'm disfigured, can she? She's left, hasn't she?"

"Eric, you couldn't be more wrong, lad," Dolly butted in. "She's in here, she collapsed last night worrying about you, she had spent every minute here by your bed. I'm afraid she lost the baby and is in a critical condition but we couldn't tell you last night because of how you were yourself," she said.

"No!" Eric cried. "I need to go to her," he said as he began trying to get out of bed.

"The nurses are going to come and sort you out and take you to see her, they were just waiting for us to tell you," Tony said, looking at his son's agonising discomfort and anguish.

Twenty minutes later Eric was in the small room where Vicky lay motionless on the bed. "Oh, my sweetheart, what has happened to us?" he said as he took her hand. He sat there and cried like a baby until he couldn't stand the pain in his face any longer. He called the nurse and she brought Eric some painkillers. He sat looking at the pale face of his beautiful wife who up until yesterday had been five months pregnant with their child. "She doesn't even know yet," he said to himself, and the tears came again. He sat there for three hours until the doctor said that he had to go and get some rest himself. He asked Eric about all the marks on Vicky's body, and he had to explain about her so-called dad and how he used to beat her.

The doctor was appalled. "I think that may be why she can't carry a child then, it explains a lot. She obviously at some point had a good kicking in her lower stomach, and it has damaged her. I'm so sorry, Mr Armstrong, but your wife will not be able to get pregnant again, as she has too much damage to her," he explained, and he left Eric to himself.

Eric was shocked. He sat down by the bed and took Vicky's hand. "That bastard has scarred you for life, inside and out," he whispered to her. "Come back to me, sweetheart, I love you so much." And he wept for himself, their lost children, and most of all for Vicky. He was taken back to his ward and told he could go back later on. Tony and Dolly came back again, and all three of them went to see Vicky.

Eric told them what the doctor had said, and they couldn't believe it. "That poor girl must have gone through hell," Tony said.

Dolly was too stunned to speak, and she quietly sobbed on Tony's shoulder. "What and how are you going to tell her when she comes round, Eric?" Dolly said softly as she put her hand on Eric's arm.

"Mom, I haven't got a clue; it's going to devastate her as much as me. I don't know what to do," he said as the tears came once again. His mom hugged him. Tony and Dolly left two hours later, Eric was allowed to stay a while longer. He sat holding Vicky's hand, talking to her and telling her how much he loved her, and that he would always be here for her to keep her safe. He talked about things they done when they were younger, told her how proud he was of her for getting through her young life as she had. The nurse came in an hour later and told him to go back to his ward and get some rest; she would come and get him if there was any change. He thanked the nurse, kissed Vicky gently on her lips and was wheeled back to his ward. The same went on for the next three days.

Then on Wednesday, the doctors told him they were going to slowly bring Vicky round, as there had been some improvement and the bleeding had been stopped for two days now, and they thought it was quite safe but she would still not be able to get out of bed for a while yet. Thursday afternoon Eric sat talking to her as usual, holding her hand, when her fingers suddenly curled around his. He looked up to see her looking at him. "Hello sweetheart, I'm here with you, don't worry," he said softly, as he could see the anguished look in her eyes. He gave her a sip of water and pressed the buzzer for the nurse.

"I've lost the baby, haven't I," she quietly said. Eric just looked at her, and before he knew it they were both crying. "How's your face, Eric?" she suddenly asked.

"It'll be fine, don't worry about that, it's you I'm worried about more than anything," he said as he squeezed her hand.

"I want to go home," she whispered.

"You can't go anywhere just yet sweetheart, you have got to get better," he said.

"I want to go home with my husband and try and return to normal," she said as she cried again.

Eric got up and hugged her. "I have the dressing off my face tomorrow so I can see just how disfigured I will be, so you might not want to go home with me," he said, smiling at her.

35

"You will still be the same Eric I married and love, nothing will ever change that," she said quietly. "Hold me, Eric, I need to feel your arms around me," she whispered. They held each other for a long while and when they finally parted, Eric kissed her gently on the lips. "I love you more than life, Vicky Armstrong; don't you ever forget that," he said.

"I know; that's why I love you so much," she whispered back.

The following day Eric had to have his dressing taken off his face. He was dreading it. "You'll be fine," Tony said to him as they waited together.

The nurse came out and called him. "Well, we'll soon see now, won't we," he smiled at his dad as he went through, dreading the outcome. Half an hour later, the nurse went out and asked Tony to come through to his son. As he went in, he looked at Eric and was horrified to see exactly what had happened to his son's face. He had a big purple scar from his left temple right down under his eye to his mouth; under the scar round his jaw line and down his neck to his collar line he was burnt, and the skin was all puckered and angry. He couldn't believe his eyes, but he tried not to let Eric see. "This is what I'm going to look like now, Dad," he said with tears in his eyes. "Disfigured and hideous."

"Don't say things like that, Son," Tony snapped at him "You are still the same person underneath," he said.

"Yes, but now I've got to go and face Vicky, and when she sees me it will make her feel sick," he said.

"No, it won't, because she loves you as much as you love her," Tony said as he put a comforting arm around his son. They finished off with the nurse and walked down to where Vicky was.

Tony went in first. "Vicky, sweetheart, Eric has had his dressing off but is worried about coming in to you because of how he looks," he told her.

"Tony, he's my husband and I love him, so that doesn't really matter to me, please tell him to come in. I've been waiting for him and I can't get up, can I?" she said, looking at him.

"Okay, but then I'm leaving you two to it," he said as he turned and went, knowing that what Eric had said about making Vicky feel sick just looking at him wouldn't come true.

Eric slowly opened the door and went in with his head down. "Eric Armstrong, will you look at me please?" Vicky said gently as she put her hand out for him. He slowly looked up, waiting for the look of horror on Vicky's face. But instead, she just looked at him and smiled, and all he could see was her love for him. "Just you remember how much I love you, and nothing will ever change that, especially not this, okay? So stop, please," she said as she pulled him to her and kissed him gently.

"Vicky sweetheart, I was so worried that I would turn your stomach with how I look now," he said as they parted.

"All I need now is to get out of here so I can go home with the husband I love and adore, okay?" she said softly as she looked up at him.

"Have you seen the doctor yet?" he asked.

"He said he was coming to see me later."

"Well, I have got something to tell you first, sweetheart," and he held her hand tight. Eric told Vicky what the doctor had said about her, and she just sat there quietly with tears running freely down her face. Eric didn't know what to do; he hated seeing her like this.

"So this means we will never have the family we wanted, because of him," she whispered through her tears. Eric just nodded as he squeezed her hand, because he could see the anguish in her face and he cried with her as they held each other. The next few hours passed as they talked and cried together.

"I'm here for you always, Vicky, no matter what, just you remember that," Eric said as he held her tightly.

She looked up at him "I know and I love you for it, I really do. I don't ever want to be without you. I love you more than anything," she said as he gently wiped the tears from her cheeks.

"Even looking like I do now," he smiled down at her.

"Even more now," she said and wrapped her arms round him, and they held each other close. Suddenly, she pulled away from him "I'll never be able to give you the children you want now," and with that she broke down again, crying her heart out, and he pulled her back to him.

"Vicky," he whispered. "We've still got each other, and that will satisfy me for the rest of my life" he said.

She pulled away from him and looked up into his eyes. "You say the most wonderful things sometimes, Eric Armstrong, but two or three years down the line you might think differently. I can't deprive you of that. You need someone who can give you the children you want. And that's not me," she said. With that, the tears rolled down her cheeks and she crumbled against him.

Eric held her tightly; he never wanted to let her go. "I'm not going anywhere, sweetheart; it's you I love and it's you I want to spend the rest of my life with. I waited long enough to get you. I'm not losing you now, not for anything," he quietly said to her.

They cried together for a while, then Vicky sat back and looked at him. She lifted her hand and gently traced the scar on his face with her fingers. "I love you more than anything, Eric, so much it hurts. I never want to be without you ever," she said as she stroked his face and kissed him. Two days later Eric was allowed home, and two weeks after that Vicky was allowed home. She had been in hospital for a nearly a month, but the doctors said she was on the mend and could go home if she had someone to look after her for a couple of weeks, as she wasn't to do anything strenuous. She and Eric had talked and cried about the things they had been told, but their love for each other was stronger than ever. Tony had brought Eric to pick her up and they were both now here in her room.

"Are you ready, sweetheart?" Eric said to her as he kissed her cheek.

"Yes, well and truly, I will be glad to get back to some sort of normality," she said.

Tony smiled at her. "And we will be glad to have you home," he said as he picked up her bags.

"Come on, Mom is waiting impatiently at home," Eric said as he put his arm around her and smiled. They had decided to stay with Tony and Dolly for a couple of weeks, as Eric was now back at work (albeit in the office) so Dolly would keep an eye on Vicky. Eric had told her that Mom and Dad knew about things, and she was relieved that they did. They arrived home just after dinner, and Dolly came out to them as they pulled up on the drive.

"Welcome home, princess," she said and gave Vicky one of her Dolly hugs.

"Thanks, it's good to be out and about again," she replied. They all made their way into the kitchen except Eric, who gently pulled Vicky into the living room first. She looked up at him and could see the longing in his eyes.

He folded his arms around her and they kissed with a passion. "I have waited over a month to do that properly to you. I've missed your touch so much," he said.

"Yes, I've missed your touch too. I long for you something terrible, do you know that?" she said as she gently kissed his cheek. With that, they both walked into the kitchen where Dolly and Tony were waiting for them. They were having a cup of tea and some of Dolly's fruit cake when Eric turned to Vicky and she smiled at him, the gorgeous smile that he hadn't seen for a while.

He took her hand and then spoke. "Mom, Dad, I've told Vicky, you know, all about things." he said gently.

"I am sorry, really I am," Dolly said as she was fighting back the tears.

"It's me who should be sorry," Vicky said quietly.

"It's okay, love, and don't you be sorry for anything, it's not your fault," she said, coming around and hugging her.

Later that evening, David called in to see them. They told him all about things, and he said the same as Dolly. The evening passed and David went home. "Well, it's time we were in bed too,"

Tony said through the kitchen door. They all said goodnight and went upstairs.

Up in the bedroom, Vicky went up behind Eric as he was getting undressed and put her arms around him. He turned and put his arms around her. They kissed longingly, but that was all they could do for now. Well, almost all! As they lay there, Eric was gently caressing Vicky's back. "I love you," he whispered in her ear as he kissed her neck.

"I love you too," she said as she turned to look at him. She cupped his chin with her fingers, then leaned over and kissed his scarred face. From then on things would be totally different, as they felt so close to each other they just melted together.

***

Two weeks later they were back in their own house and the wanting in them both had increased to an all-time high. Come 9 pm, all their visitors had gone and at last they were totally alone. Eric scooped Vicky up in his arms and carried her up the stairs. "You sure everything's okay now?" he said as he put her gently on the bed.

"It couldn't be better; the doctor said I'm good to go," she smiled up at him as she started undoing the belt on his trousers. He gently took off her blouse and bra, all the time kissing her breasts and neck. She slipped off her panties, and he took off his trousers and everything else. They toured each other's bodies with their hands as if it were their first time. They kissed each other all over and brought each other to a wanting like never before. Eric very gently entered her, but neither could suppress the need for each other. They made love on and off for the next three hours until they reached the passion that had been kept in for seven weeks. It was heaven for them both, exploding against each other, gripping each others' bodies.

***

"Would you like me to make you something to eat?" Vicky said to Eric as he lay on the settee one afternoon.

"What I would like is for you to come and lie on here with me," he said as he pulled her down to him. "Everything will be all right now, sweetheart," he said as she lay down next to him and smiled the smile she had when she was happy.

"I know, because we have each other and my love for you will never die," she whispered. They kissed and Vicky snuggled up to him and they lay the rest of the afternoon cocooned in each other and watching the TV. Eric was healing well and things would start to get back to normal. They could both fully return back to work, and life would go on. Eric's thirtieth birthday and their fourth wedding anniversary were coming up.

One night as they lay in bed after they had loved each other up again, Eric said to her, "Are you happy, sweetheart? I mean truly happy?"

Vicky looked up at him and kissed him. "Yes, I am. I couldn't ask for anything more as long as I have you," she said.

"Shall we have a party, then?" he said suddenly as he hugged her.

"Well, with our anniversary and your thirtieth, I don't see why not," she said, hugging him back.

They started making plans for everything. They were going to invite everyone they knew, including all of Eric's staff. With just two months to go, Vance came to see them at their house one night. "Hello, Vance," Eric said as he answered the door. "This is a nice surprise, what's up?"

"Nothing at all, lad," Vance smiled as he went through to the living room where Vicky was. He hugged her and kissed her cheek. "Hello, angel, how are you doing?"

"I'm well, thank you."

They all sat down and Vance smiled at them both. "Well, I will tell you why I'm here when you have got me a large whisky, my lad," he said to Eric, grinning.

"Certainly, me lord," Eric laughed.

"It's nice to see you again, Vance," Vicky said as Eric handed them both a drink. "I haven't seen you for a while, with one thing and another; are you okay?"

"Yes, I'm good, thank you, but I've got something to put to you both; that's why I came," he said as he took a large gulp of his whisky.

"Sounds a bit ominous for you," Eric said as he smiled across at Vicky.

"Well, as you know, I look upon you two as family, as I haven't any. I've known you both since the day you were born, and love you both as if you were my own," he said, taking another gulp of his whisky and emptying his glass.

"Another?" Eric asked.

"You know me, lad, of course I'll have another," he smiled. "Anyway, as I was saying, I couldn't ask to be involved with a nicer, happier couple, and would be made up if you would let me throw you your party at my house," he said. Eric and Vicky looked at each other. amazed. "I've got that big house all to myself and it hasn't seen any enjoyment in it for years, and I would love it if you would let me do it for you both, anything you want. Vicky, I would leave it all for you to arrange but don't spare anything, as you know I have enough money for anything so the world is your oyster, my angel," he said, grinning at them.

Eric knew exactly what Vicky was thinking, and knew that he could answer for her without asking her, because she loved Vance's house. "Well, that would be wonderful, Vance, thank you," Eric said as he looked over at Vicky.

Vicky got up and hugged him. "Thank you, you have made my day, you know how I love your house," she said, kissing his cheek.

"Yes, that's what I thought," he said. "So can I leave it all to you to sort out and, like I said, I am paying for it all and don't scrimp on anything, right?" he said warmly.

***

Everything was planned to perfection and on 11 June 1989, Eric and Vicky had a party they would never forget. They were staying the weekend with Vance; he had given them one of the master bedrooms in his mansion and had been the perfect host as they knew he would be, because he was the perfect gentleman and they loved him as he loved them. They were up in their room that afternoon and Eric came up behind Vicky as she was undressing to get in the shower. "Would you like me to join you, Mrs Armstrong?" he said as he kissed her neck.

"No, you can behave yourself for once, Mr Armstrong, and get yourself ready instead. The guests will be arriving in less than an hour," she said as she turned around and kissed his cheek.

"Spoilsport" he said as he kissed her nose and walked over to the wardrobe. Vicky went into the en suite and got into the shower, smiling. Before she knew it, Eric was in the shower behind her. "I couldn't resist you, sweetheart, sorry," he said as he put his arms around her and kissed her shoulders and back.

She promptly turned around and put her arms around his neck; she could feel his need against her hip and it aroused her further. He lifted her up as they kissed and she wrapped her legs around him. With her back against the shower wall, he entered her and her legs wrapped round him tighter, They made love there and then in the shower and it was heaven; he was her gentle giant and she loved him. They stilled and just stood together, getting their breath. "I love you, Vicky" he whispered as he looked down at her.

"I know," she said as she reached up and kissed his scarred cheek. "I love you too." Half an hour later they were getting dressed. Vicky had brought a new dress especially for the occasion; it was blood-red with lace sleeves and a low-cut lace bodice, and fitted her slim body to perfection, hiding her scars beneath.

Eric walked out of the bathroom. "Jesus, Vicky, you look wonderful, I could eat you all over again looking like that. You know what you're going to be doing to me all night, don't you?"

he said as he went and put his arms around her and tenderly kissed her.

"That was the whole idea of wearing it," she said, smiling. "Just to tease you so you behave yourself tonight."

"Oh, believe me, I will if this is what I've got to come back to later, definitely not too much drink. I think I will be needing my stamina too much for you later." They both burst out laughing.

"I love you so much, Eric," Vicky said as she softly kissed his lips.

"I know and I love you just as much."

***

Ten minutes later they went downstairs, and the guests started arriving. Everyone turned up and they even had a marquee in the garden and a BBQ, as the weather was perfect and the caterers had done wonders.

Vance came up to Vicky and put his arm around her. "You look absolutely amazing tonight, Vicky. Are you enjoying yourself, angel?" he said to her. Vance knew of the trauma she had been through because he too knew about "daddy dearest."

"Yes I am, it's wonderful, thank you, and thank you for being you and doing all this for us," she said, and promptly kissed his cheek. "Now I am going to go and find the birthday boy and tell him I want a dance," she laughed as she went. She found Eric with David propping up the bar in the marquee.

"Here comes trouble," David said, laughing as he spotted her.

"Oi, you watch it, else I'll tell Cora where you are," she grinned.

Eric promptly put his arms around her and kissed her. "How's my girl enjoying herself?" he said.

"It's wonderful," she said as she kissed him back.

"Where's Cora then?" David asked as he moved away from the bar.

"Last I saw of her she was in the house talking to Leo," Vicky replied. At that, David went in search of his wife. Cora was now eight months pregnant and David couldn't wait. Unfortunately, Vicky had noticed that Cora wasn't the same as David. She had become a cold fish towards her husband, but Vicky didn't know if it was just because of the baby. "Eric, have you noticed how Cora has become towards David," Vicky asked whilst they were standing by the bar.

"Yes, I have noticed lately that she doesn't like being with him much, but maybe it's because of the way she is at the moment," he said, smiling down at her.

"Maybe," Vicky said but wasn't convinced. The party was great. Dolly had one too many sherries and started singing, and Tony had to put her to bed. They were also staying the weekend. Cora seemed like she was just tolerating David, but kept good company with Leo. Leo was Eric's foreman and a good one at that, even though he wasn't very well-liked. His wife was something else, though. All night she kept staring at Eric.

Her eyes followed him everywhere, and Eric had noticed and so had David. "I see you have noticed how Monica's eyes are following you everywhere," David said to Eric as he noticed him cringing as she looked at him yet again.

"Yes, but I don't think it's anything like that, I think it's just because of my face," he replied, turning and walking over to Vicky.

David followed him. "Don't go getting upset, mate, take no notice, just look at what you have got here," he said, nodding his head towards Vicky, who was talking to Vance. "She looks stunning tonight, I'll say that much. You're a lucky bloke, you know, Eric," he said as they went up the bar.

"Yes, I know, but I really thought I'd lost her when this happened, and losing the baby," he said, putting his hand up to his face.

"Yes, but you two have a special bond and I only wish I had that with Cora," David said sadly.

"Are you two having problems, then?" Eric asked.

"You could say that. I really thought that having this baby would bring us back together, but it's had the opposite effect, she spends as little time with me as possible. I think she regrets getting pregnant because it wasn't planned," he said, looking over to where Cora was laughing at something Leo had said.

"She spends a lot of time with Leo though, doesn't she?" Eric said as he looked over to where David was looking.

"Yes. I don't really like him. I know he's good at his job and all but he's so smarmy with it, isn't he?" David replied.

"Yes, you could say that, but with a wife like his I'm not surprised. Vicky doesn't like either of them; finds them both a bit obnoxious," Eric said as he got their drinks.

"Come on, let's go over to Vicky and Vance; least they are good company," David said as he turned and walked over to where they were.

"Well, look at who's decided to join us," Vance said, smiling at them both. "Your lovely wife has been keeping me company, Eric, but I think she may be slightly distracted by a certain person here," he said, looking at Vicky.

"Yes, and we bet we know who it is, too," David said, looking at Eric.

"Is everything okay, sweetheart?" Eric asked Vicky, looking worried.

"Yes, fine," she answered, reaching up and kissing his cheek. She then looked round and saw Monica staring at her with a look of disgust on her face. Eric noticed what she was looking at and also saw the look of disgust on Monica's face, but didn't say anything.

The evening went on and all was well until Monica had had one too many drinks. She started slagging off Cora for hogging her husband and then she quietly started on Vicky. "How can you kiss a face like that?" she hissed in Vicky's ear as she passed her through the people dancing. Vicky just stood there, amazed.

She did no more but follow Monica into the bathroom. "And just what do you mean by that comment?" she asked Monica when she had closed the door behind her.

"Well look at you, wanting for nothing but with an ugly scarface for a husband, how you can wake up looking at that every morning amazes me, enough to give you nightmares. It would make me want to puke to have to kiss that," she said nastily.

"Well, you will never get the chance to, thank God, and at least Eric has some decorum, not like your husband who is continuously flirting with my sister-in-law. No wonder he ignores the nasty piece of work he married," she said, and turned and walked out of the bathroom. She returned to the party but didn't realise that David and Vance had seen them both go in and saw just how shaken Vicky was when she came out.

"Are you okay, Vicky?" David asked as he went over to her and put his arm round her shoulder.

"Yes, I'm fine thanks, where's Eric?" she said shakily.

"At this present moment, I don't think you should let him see you like this," he said.

"I totally agree," Vance piped in. "We saw what just happened, Vicky, and we know why. I'll get you a brandy, angel," Vance said, and disappeared to the bar.

Just then Eric came over to them. "Hey, you trying to steal my wife, brother? Hands off," he laughed, but then sensed something was wrong. "Vicky, you okay sweetheart?"

"Yes, I'm fine, just can't stand that woman," she said as she nodded towards Monica swaying across the room. She told David and Vance what she had said, and they couldn't believe it. The situation didn't get much better because David caught Cora and Leo kissing and groping behind the marquee and threatened to kill him.

Eric stepped in and told Leo he was sacked, and to stay away from Cora. "We'll see," Leo slurred out. But before he could say any more Monica was there, and she slapped Cora across the face and thumped her husband. Eric promptly threw the pair of them out and told them he never wanted to see either of them again. David didn't know what to do. His heavily pregnant wife was stone cold sober but kissing and groping another man. One thing was clear: it had cleared his mind as to his situation with Cora.

"I think that I need to have a serious talk with that bloody wife of mine," David said quietly to Eric once all the fuss had died down. "Do you know where she went?"

"I think she went upstairs," Eric said. With that, David went in search of his wife to tell her a few home truths. "It's a good job Mom and Dad have already gone up," Eric said to Vicky as he put his arm round her. "You okay sweetheart? You look pale," he said, concerned.

"Yes, I'm okay, I've got you and I love you more than ever tonight and nothing can spoil that," she said, and promptly kissed him gently on his lips.

"Mm, you can do that as much as you like, you taste good," he said as he hugged her and she smiled up at him.

"It's David I feel sorry for, he was really looking forward to this baby and Cora has spoilt everything for him," she said as she put her head on his shoulder.

Just then, Vance came over. "Everything's back to normal, excitement's been forgotten. I didn't realise how many people disliked those two, and everyone is glad they have gone. You okay, angel," he asked Vicky, looking at Eric.

"Yes, I'm fine thanks, my gorgeous husband has a calming effect on me," she said, kissing Eric as he smiled down at her. Vance looked at them both and smiled. He knew the bond between them was a strong one, and he loved them both for it, as he knew just how much they loved each other.

Come midnight everyone was beginning to depart, thanking Vicky and Eric for a wonderful evening and not mentioning the fuss. When everyone had gone, Vance drew them both into the sitting room. "Well, that was a great night. I have enjoyed myself immensely. I just hope that poor David can sort himself out," he said. "Can I get you both a night cap before you go up?"

"That would be great, Vance, thanks," Eric said as he and Vicky sat on the enormous soft leather settee. Vance gave them both a large brandy and they sat chatting for a while.

"I think I'm going up now," Vance said about half an hour later.

"I think we will be following you," Vicky said, yawning. Once they were upstairs in their room, Vicky did no more than wrap her arms around Eric's neck and kissed him like there was no tomorrow.

"Wow," he said, looking down at her and smiling. "Have you been saving that up all night, or is there more where that came from?" he said as he unzipped the back of her dress.

"Oh, there's plenty more, Mr Armstrong, I just hope you are up to it," she said teasingly as she started to undo his shirt.

"Well, in that case I better warn you that, because I have had to look at you all night in that dress and knowing what's underneath it, you had better be prepared too, madam," he whispered as he kissed her neck. The thought of what Monica had said to Vicky went through her head and it made her kiss Eric hard and meaningfully. It made her hungry for him. How dare she say what she said about him! Vicky loved him with a passion and she would protect him from the nastiness of people all she could. They undressed each other and teased each other to distraction.

Eric picked her up and lay her on the huge bed. He kissed her with butterfly kisses all over, caressing her breasts and kissing her nipples, bringing her to dizzy heights. All the time she was caressing him and making him groan with lust for her. "Jesus, Vic, I need you," he whispered as he kissed her neck. He eventually entered her when neither of them could hold on any longer, but still they did, slowing and kissing as they couldn't get enough of each other and they just melted together, enjoying each others' bodies until the moment of satisfaction erupted in both of them and they both bonded together. Afterwards they lay entwined together in bed, and Vicky felt as if her heart would burst with love for this man.

Eric lay with his arms around her, caressing her back and feeling as if he had been given a love so strong it was unimaginable. He didn't know the power of love could be so strong. It was nearly 3.30 am before they fell to sleep encased in each others' arms.

"No, please stop, it hurts," she shouted. Eric was awake in seconds, wrapping his arms around Vicky, gluing her to him. She was shaking and sobbing into his chest. The sobs slowly subsided.

"It's okay, sweetheart, let it out, I'm here," he said gently as he held on to her.

She slowly looked up at him, her face streaked with tears. "Oh, Eric, I love you so very much," she said and buried her face back into his chest.

"I know," he whispered.

***

Early the next morning, Eric was woken by Vicky kissing his chest and working her way down towards his stomach. "Oh Vicky," he murmured, and lay there gently stroking her body whilst she aroused him and teased him even further. She eased herself upon him and, once again, the sex they had was out of this world. God, how he loved this woman. Two hours later they went downstairs after showering together and dressing. Vance had his housekeeper in, and she had cooked the most delicious breakfast. David came down alone.

"Morning, how's things this morning?" Eric asked, concerned by the way David looked.

"I'll speak to you later because Mom and Dad are on their way down and I don't want to say anything yet," he said quietly. Eric patted his shoulder and nodded.

"Good morning," everyone said as Dolly and Tony came in.

"What's good about it?" Dolly said groggily. "I feel awful," she said, holding her head.

"That'll teach you to lay off the sherry," Eric laughed, and everyone joined him.

"Okay, okay, I know it's my own fault, but I enjoyed it so I don't care," she said indignantly, but smiling. They all sat and ate breakfast, talking about the night before, except for the one problem they had had.

"Where's Cora?" Dolly suddenly asked.

Everyone looked at each other. "She's stayed in bed for a bit, Mom," David lied.

"Oh, okay, she's all right though, isn't she?" she asked.

"Yes, she's fine," he said, lying once more. Eric looked across at David and could see the anguish in his eyes. "I think I will go up and see how she is," he said, and as he got up he nodded towards the door to Eric.

Vicky saw what he done and promptly said to David, "Do you want me to come and see her? She might appreciate a woman's touch." She looked up at David and raised her eyebrows.

"Yes, she probably would, thanks Vicky," he said, and with that he was gone.

Vicky got up and squeezed Eric's hand as she did so; he understood this. As they went up the stairs David turned to Vicky and he had tears in his eyes. "She's leaving me, Vicky, she says she doesn't want the baby. She's going off with that bloody Leo of all people, they have been seeing each other for the last seven months. I must be blind or bloody stupid," he said sadly. They got to David's room and he opened the door.

"What the hell do you want now?" Cora spat as she looked up from packing her bag.

"Cora, surely you can sort this out, even just for the baby's sake," Vicky said pleadingly.

"Oh I thought you might come and state your case," she snarled at Vicky. "Miss bloody perfect with her perfect life and a husband who's got a face like a map. God, I hate all of you, you're pathetic," she sneered.

"How dare you say that about Eric? He's been good to you," Vicky said as she shut the door behind her so those downstairs wouldn't hear what was going on, especially Eric. David couldn't believe what he was hearing. He knew that he and Cora were now finished, but he couldn't believe how vindictive she was being towards his family, especially Vicky and Eric.

"Cora, mind what you are saying, we have never done anything against you," Vicky said.

"No, of course you haven't, little miss bloody perfect you are, aren't you, with your ragged body and your. nightly screaming, just wonderful, aren't you. You two make a good pair together, like a couple of maps. Well, at least I will have a man that doesn't look like a freak show or one that's as boring as hell," she said, looking at David. "At least Leo is a master in the bedroom and he knows how to excite me," she scowled at David. With that, she zipped up her bag and headed towards the door.

"Is the baby mine, Cora?" David asked quietly.

"Oh yes, the bloody thing's yours all right, that much I do know, and when it's born you can bloody well keep it," she said, opening the door.

"How can you be so callous and cruel?" Vicky said as she passed her.

"Oh, shut your fucking mouth, you. At least I can have kids and I'm not barren like you. There again, who would want scarface as a dad? Scare a baby to death, that would." Vicky visibly blanched and David saw it, he also saw rage creep into Vicky's eyes, something he had never seen. Cora turned and left the room. She went down the stairs at a speed quite unlike a heavily pregnant woman.

"Cora," David shouted and ran out of the room after her.

"What you want now?' she said as she turned and looked up at him.

"Will you let me know when you go in to have it?" he said with tears running down his face.

"Oh, you will know all right, because you will be the one taking the bloody brat home with you, not me," she shouted at him. "Ask her behind you to look after it because she can't manage to have any of her own, can she, the stupid cow, and she calls herself a woman? Scarface and your mother will spoil it rotten like she has with all of you, bloody mommy's boys," she spat out and continued down the stairs.

By this time, everyone was out of the dining room and standing in the hallway, having heard the commotion. Eric couldn't believe what he was hearing, but he could see his wife and his brother standing at the top of the stairs with tears running down their faces, and he was livid. "Leave my house right now before I throw you out myself," Vance shouted at her.

"Oh yes, old man, you would like to manhandle a woman, wouldn't you. I also know you would like to get your hands on her," she said, pointing up at Vicky "Have her as your fancy bit, wouldn't you, if she'd have you, you old pervert. But she'd rather have a scar-faced freak as a husband, than a sugar daddy. You make me sick, all of you."

With that she turned toward the door, but before she could get it open or anybody had time to do anything Vicky flew down the stairs, pushing past David, and grabbed her by the shoulders, spinning her round and slapping her face so quick and hard even Cora didn't see it coming. "How dare you talk about any of us like that, you bitch? It's you that's been acting like a tart and upsetting everyone, and you don't deserve that child in you anyway. You're despicable. Go on, get out and never come back. You and bloody Leo deserve each other; you're both scum. I hope you rot in hell for what you have done. He'll only do the dirty on you as well anyway, because that's what he is and I hope he does; you'll deserve it. He's a bastard and always will be, and you're nothing but a cruel heartless bitch." Vicky shouted at her.

"Well well, Little Miss Perfect has lost her temper all because I called her old man scarface and insulted his family. You make me sick, all of you," Cora said rubbing her face as she looked round at them all. "You'll pay for this, BITCH, and don't forget it," she hissed in Vicky's face.

By now Eric was at Vicky's side, and he opened the door and near enough shoved Cora out of it. "Bye everybody," she said sarcastically. "Oh, and Vicky dearest, don't forget I owe you a slapping, bitch, and I won't fucking forget, okay?" Eric slammed the door shut behind her.

Vicky stood there visibly shaking from head to toe. Eric wrapped his arms around her and just stood holding her. He looked over her head towards his mother, who was comforting David, then to Vance and his father, who still hadn't moved. Suddenly, Vance came to his senses. "I will go and get some strong coffee sorted, will everyone come into the sitting room for some?" he asked as he went towards the kitchen.

"Yes," Dolly said as she came down the stairs with David and went into the sitting room with him and Tony.

"I'm sorry for that," Vicky whispered as she held Eric.

"Hey, you've got nothing to be sorry for," he said as he cupped her chin with his hand and kissed her. "At least I know how people see me now, as if I didn't know already," he said, smiling down at her.

Vicky kissed him gently. "Well, not me, to me you're my gorgeous husband and you always will be because I love you," she said, putting her head on his chest.

"Are you okay now? I've never seen you like that before; nobody has, come to that. I think that's what shocked everyone," he said.

"Well, I've never had to defend my own before, have I?" She smiled up at him as they went towards the sitting room.

"Remind me never to upset you, then," he laughed.

"As if you could or would," she replied.

They entered the sitting room to see David sitting as if in shock. He got up when they went in, and came over to Vicky and put his arms around her. "I'm sorry, David," she said as she held him.

"Thank you, Vicky, you only said to her what I hadn't got the balls to say, but I have never seen you anything like that before, you were wild," he said as he stood back and smiled at her.

"Exactly what I said, brother, she's got a dark side to her," Eric laughed, trying to lighten the situation.

"Don't ever upset her then," David laughed back. Just then Vance entered the room with a tray of coffee, looking rather pale. Vicky went over to him, took the tray off him and put it on the coffee table. She then put her arms around him and kissed his cheek. "Stop looking so worried, I don't believe a word she said. I've known you too long to think any different," she said to him.

Eric looked over at his wife. He was so proud of her, she was amazing. Vance had to sit down on the chair. "Vicky, my child, all I have ever seen in you is that you are the daughter I never had," he said quietly.

"We know that, Vance," Tony said. "We all do and nothing would ever change that, I promise you, I've known you nearly all my life, just a bit longer than she has," he smiled at him.

"Well, all I know is that at the moment she has crucified my son and gone off to God knows where expecting my grandchild," Dolly said rather huffily.

"Mom, all will end well, believe me," Eric said as he put an arm round Vicky. They carried on discussing the situation for hours, with Vance's housekeeper making sandwiches for them all and then supper.

They all retired back to the sitting room and had a drink before bed. "You, young lady, need to get some rest," Tony said to Vicky, who had suddenly gone very quiet. Eric noticed his dad's look of concern at Vicky.

"Are you okay, sweetheart?" he asked, looking down at her.

She looked up at him with eyes brimming with tears. "Yes, I just need to go to bed I think," she said.

Eric understood what his precious wife was saying. She wanted them to be on their own. "Right then, we will sort this in the morning when everyone's got a clear head," Eric said as he moved towards the door holding Vicky's hand.

"We'll talk in the morning," Vicky said quietly to David as she gave him a hug.

"Good night," everyone said as they all made their way upstairs.

Once they were in their room, Eric did no more than wrap his arms around his wife. "Are you sure you're okay, sweetheart?" he said as he looked down at her.

Vicky wrapped her arms around his neck and kissed him longingly on his lips. "At this present moment all I am sure about is that I want you more than anything. Take me to bed and have your wicked way with me, my wonderful sweet lover," she said, looking up into his deep blue eyes.

"Mm, well, I think I can help you out there, and thanks for the compliment, gorgeous," he smiled at her as he started undoing her blouse. Vicky undid Eric's shirt and then trousers while he was undressing her. He lifted her onto the bed and they caressed each other willingly. They made love passionately, feeling that they never wanted it to end, embracing each others' feelings and emotions. They collapsed into each other, trying to catch their breath but all the time not wanting to let go. All Vicky wanted now was her husband next to her with his strong arms around her, protecting her. But afterwards, as they lay entangled in each other, all she could think of was what Cora had said to her, calling her a bitch and saying she would get a slapping. Surely she didn't mean it! Did she?

The following day after discussing the situation from the night before, everyone went home. David went back to his mom and dad's until things were sorted with his house, because as of yet he didn't know where Cora had gone and he didn't want to see her.

CHAPTER FOUR

During the next three weeks David sorted his house. It was up for sale with Cora getting just ten percent of the selling price because of her adultery, and because she wasn't keeping their baby. David had been to a solicitor and had papers drawn up for her to sign, saying that she had given sole custody of their baby to David with no visitation rights. She just wanted to cut herself off completely. He had had two visits off Leo's wife to see if he knew where they were, but he didn't, not until he had a phone call late one evening from Cora herself. "Just to let you know that I'm in hospital and by morning I should have had your brat, okay" she sneered down the phone.

After her telling him which hospital she was in, he phoned his mom and dad and Eric and Vicky. "We'll see you there," they both said, and he changed and set off for the hospital. When he got there the others were already there waiting for him.

"Your mom has sorted out where she is," Tony said as he walked in.

"Yes, well, I'm not going in anyway. I will wait for the nurse to come and tell us what's what," he said solemnly.

Vicky went up to him and hugged him. "We're all here for you and we will all help you. Just think of yourself now and that little mite in there," she said as she kissed his cheek.

"Thanks, Vicky, I know you will. I couldn't ask for a better sister in law you know," he said as he looked at her. Three hours later, on 12 July 1989, David's little son was born weighing in at seven pounds eight ounces. David was ecstatic.

"Do you have a name for him yet" Eric asked him as he shook his hand.

"Yes, Thomas," David replied.

"After Granddad Thomas?" Eric asked, smiling at him.

"Yes, well, I thought I would keep it in the family," he said with a smile on his face that would put a Cheshire cat to shame.

"Ooh, I'm a grandma," Dolly said, beside herself with joy.

David went and put his arms around Vicky. "Are you okay, Vicky?" He couldn't even begin to think what she was feeling, as she could never have children and he felt so desperately sorry for her because she would have made someone a wonderful mom.

"Yes, I'm fine thanks, I'm so happy for you David, just sorry the circumstances couldn't be better for you," she smiled at him.

"Yes, well, better to find out now rather than another couple of years down the line when Tom would have known his mom. At least this way he never has to know her unless he wants to when he's older," he said.

"Mm, I can see what you mean. So are we going to be calling him Tom then, not Thomas?" she asked, laughing.

"Do you know I just automatically said that then, so yes, Tom it is then, but Thomas will be his full name," he laughed.

Just then Eric came over from talking with his mom and dad. "What are you two up to over here?" he said as he put his arm around Vicky and she kissed his cheek.

"David has just decided that our little nephew will be known to everyone as Tom, I think it's really sweet," she said, looking up at Eric.

"Women, they always go sloppy over babies, don't they?" Eric said as he hugged her and looked over at David and smiled.

David laughed. "Yes, all apart from his own mother," he said.

Two days later they took little Tom home. When everyone was settled with food and drink, Vicky went and sat by David in the conservatory, where he was looking down at his tiny son in his carry cot. "How did everything go at the hospital with Cora when you fetched him?" she asked.

"Oh, she was just the same vindictive Cora that she has turned into, wasn't the slightest bit bothered about just handing her own son over, heartless bitch that she is," he said. What he didn't tell Vicky was that she had also reminded him that she would get her own back on Vicky for slapping her in front of everyone and that Vicky and Scarface, what she called Eric now, would pay dearly for what they had done to her.

Later that night, when Vicky and Eric were home and getting ready for bed, Eric put his arms around her and kissed her gently on her lips. "I love you, you okay?" he said as he unzipped her dress.

"Yes, I'm fine," she said as she kissed him back and put her arms around his neck. "Are you okay?" she asked him.

"As long as I've got you I couldn't ask to be happier," he said as he lifted her onto the bed. Eric was leaning over her on the bed, looking into her eyes, and she lifted her hand and stroked his face. "Do you know just how much I love you?" he whispered as he kissed her hand and then her neck.

"No, I don't really, you will have to show me," she whispered back as she pulled him to her. They made love twice that night, each time with a passion for each other like never before, exploring each other's bodies over and over, reaching their heights together and not being able to get enough of each other. They collapsed into each other and fell to sleep spooned together.

***

Over the next few weeks, things settled down and Tom started to fill out a treat. Dolly had him every day while David went to work, and they fell into a routine that suited them all. One Friday night when they had all congregated round Mom and Dad's house, David let them all know some good news. "I'm buying a house," he said, looking around and smiling at everyone, "and before you all ask, yes, it's local to everybody," he said.

Eric sat there smiling too, because he had been in on helping him get it, and so had Vance. "Well, are you going to tell us where it is then?" Dolly piped up.

"Yes, it's between the Golden Thistle and Eric and Vicky's house, in fact it's three doors down from Eric's but across the road and its great," he beamed.

"Well, son, I knew you would get there and it wouldn't take you long, good for you, lad," Tony said proudly.

"Don't worry, Mom, I will still be bringing Tom to you three times a week, and Vicky is going to have him three times a week too, because then I can still work for five days and still have a night out too," David said as he looked around the room at everyone.

"Oh David, I'm so proud of the way you have picked yourself up after that trollop of a wife of yours let you down," Dolly said with tears in her eyes, going over and hugging him. David and Vicky smiled at each other and Eric winked at Vicky. They had done all this between them to help sort David out and to keep Dolly happy with her grandson.

"Well, when will all this be happening then?" Tony asked.

"The house is all going through now, I wanted to be certain that I'd got it before I said anything though, but its all going okay so I should be able to move in within two weeks because its already empty. The owners have moved abroad and they have left all their furniture so I have bought that too, in the price of the house," David told everyone.

"Well, this calls for a celebration drink, I reckon," Tony said as he opened the drinks cabinet and got out the glasses.

"Too true, it does," Eric agreed.

"I know you two have helped David in all this and I'm really proud of you all," Dolly whispered to Vicky.

Vicky turned around and hugged her mother-in-law. "Yes, well, we had to, didn't we? We couldn't see him struggle on his own, and having Tom all week is getting too much for you now, and when he starts crawling about it will be even harder for you to keep up with him. I know how you have been suffering with your arthritis and your angina and things, even if the lads don't know. You should tell them, you know, what the doctor has said to you, because they would never forgive you if anything happens," Vicky said quietly to Dolly.

"I know and I will when the time is right, I promise. I know you don't like keeping things from Eric and I know I'm asking a lot from you to keep this from him, but I promise by Monday I will tell them," she said as she kissed Vicky's cheek and hugged her.

"Right, everybody, have you all got a drink?" Tony said. "Here's to our David's new house and new start with Tom, best of luck, Son," he said, and they all cheered.

That night, when Vicky and Eric got home, Eric was really quiet. "Are you okay, sweetheart?" Vicky said as she put her arms round him in the kitchen.

"Yes, I'm okay, I'm just worried that you might go off me now that David is moving closer with Tom. You will be seeing a lot of him and the baby and it's what you have always wanted," he said, looking down at her.

Vicky took a step back in amazement at what she was hearing. "Eric Armstrong, I have never heard anything so absurd in all my life. How can you even think of anything like that? I love you, you idiot," she said as she gently stroked his scarred face with her fingers "And nothing or no one will ever change that," she whispered as she kissed his cheek.

"I'm sorry, Vicky, I know I shouldn't have said that, but I saw you both together tonight and you get on so well, and I know what David has always thought of you," he said.

"Eric, David is a lovely man and my brother-in-law at that, but at this present moment I want his big brother to take me to bed with him and do what he does to me so well," she whispered in his ear as she started kissing his neck and unbuttoning his shirt.

"Oh God, Vicky, how could I have even thought it when you do these things to me? I'm sorry," he said as he started hardening at her touch.

"Shush, don't talk, just be the you I love and want," she breathed onto his chest as she started undoing his trousers.

By now Eric had her blouse off and her skirt down her ankles. He lifted her onto the edge of the kitchen table as she wrapped her long legs around him. She pulled his shirt off him and kissed his chest, working her way up to his mouth. "Jesus, Vicky, I love you so much," he said as he caressed her breasts. They groaned with sheer delight at the touch of each others' bodies. Eric entered her with a passion so hot it took both their breaths away. Vicky lay back on the table pulling Eric with her, and that's where they had sex with red hot passion for each other, the bed forgotten.

That night after they had gone to bed, Vicky was awakened by Eric gently caressing her body. She turned and kissed him gently on the lips, and he in turn slid down the bed and started kissing her breasts. She was instantly aroused for him yet again and he for her, and they made love gently and longingly with each other, no words needed.

***

Monday morning came and Vicky had all intentions of going to see Dolly, but that morning she had a letter through the post that disturbed her greatly. HELLO VICKY, DON'T FORGET THAT YOUR DAY IS COMING. YOU WILL NOT KNOW WHAT HAS HIT YOU AND THAT FREAK LOOKING HUSBAND OF YOURS WILL BE LEFT WITH ABSOLUTELY NOTHING. IT WILL SERVE YOU BOTH RIGHT YOU BASTARDS. Vicky had to sit down when she read it, she knew exactly who it was from but had no proof of it. What could she do? She couldn't tell Eric and David because they would find her and God knows what they would do. But at the same time this would be another secret she would keep from Eric and she hated doing it. In the end she hid the letter and tried to carry on as usual.

She got to Dolly's and tried her hardest to forget it and concentrate on Dolly. "Have you decided what you are going to say to everyone?" she asked as Dolly poured some coffee.

"I haven't thought of anything else," she said as she sat down at the kitchen table with Vicky. "I know I have put a lot on you by asking you not to say anything and keeping it from Eric because I know you two are so open with each other, but you were the only person I could tell because you are like a daughter to me. I couldn't confide in anyone else. Do you understand what I mean?" she said as she put her hand over Vicky's.

"Yes, I think I do, but you must tell them tonight when they are both here, and it will take a load off your mind because I can see you worrying and it's not doing you any favours," Vicky said gently to her.

"I'm going to, I promise," she said, sipping her coffee. "Anyway, enough about me, what's worrying you? Because don't forget, I know you too well and I can see something's up because it's not like you," Dolly said, getting up.

Vicky could in no way tell Dolly the truth; she couldn't tell anyone. "I'm worried about you, of course, and just how you are going to cope for three days with Tom," Vicky lied.

"We will just have to see how I get on," Dolly said, sitting back down with more coffee. Later that afternoon, everyone started getting back from work. They were all coming for tea. So Vicky had helped Dolly prepare everything and get it all ready, as they had been looking after Tom for David and had had a really lovely afternoon. Eric got back about five o'clock and came straight over to Vicky, giving her a kiss.

"Can we go into the living room a minute?" he whispered as he kissed her cheek. They sidled out of the kitchen whilst everyone was talking.

"What's the matter?" Vicky asked, looking worried as Eric closed the door behind him.

"Nothing," he smiled down at her as he put his arms around her. "I just wanted my wife to myself for a couple of minutes so I could tell her how much I love her and have missed her like hell today," he said as he kissed her lips.

"You are terrible, Eric Armstrong," Vicky said as she responded willingly to his kiss. "Everyone will be wondering where we have gone," she said as she pulled herself away.

"They will be okay for a couple of minutes, I just wish we could lock the door because you do things to me at the most strangest of times," he said, pulling her back to him, and she could feel his hardness against her and wanted him too. "I think we had better get back before we forget ourselves," Eric smiled down at her, kissing her nose.

"I think you had better wait until I've gone in and follow me," Vicky laughed.

Eric knew exactly what she meant, as he was hard for her and couldn't really walk into his mom's kitchen like that. As they were all gathered round in the dining room, Dolly made her stance. "I have something to tell you all," she said as she looked over at Vicky. "I've been to the doctors and I've been for some tests and I've got to go and have an operation on my heart," she said as she looked round at everyone.

Tony sat there knowing that this was the worst thing his wife had had to do. Telling her kids. He, like Vicky, had known from the start, and the worry of it all was crucifying him. But Vicky had been a rock to him as well as Dolly, and he knew that she had hated keeping it from Eric. "What have you got to have done, Mom?" David asked quietly.

"I've got to have a bypass. It will be okay' it's just that with my angina there may be a small risk," she said.

"When are you going in?" Eric said as he walked round the table and hugged his mom.

"Next week on Tuesday. I've been dreading telling you all, but that's why I wanted you all together today," she said. They all sat and talked about everything for the next hour or so, and everything was sorted for when Dolly went into hospital the following week.

When Vicky and Eric got home that night, Eric turned to Vicky and said, "You knew, didn't you, about Mom." Vicky just looked up at him. "I thought we didn't have secrets from each other. When did we stop being open with one another and hiding things?" he said as he walked into the kitchen.

Vicky sat down on the sofa and began to cry. Eric had never walked off from her like that before; what would he do if he knew she had kept the letter secret as well? She couldn't tell him, though. She sat with her head in her hands and sobbed, not only for upsetting Eric but for knowing she was hurting him again without him even knowing it. Suddenly, Vicky felt Eric's arms go round her. She looked up and he was kneeling in front of her. "Oh God, I'm sorry sweetheart, I didn't mean to upset you, let alone make you cry. I know you would have told me if you hadn't had to promise Mom that you wouldn't. Please don't cry," he said as he wiped a tear off her cheek with his fingertips and gently kissed her lips.

"I'm sorry too," she said as she looked into his eyes. But she was more sorry for what she wasn't telling him now. A week later Dolly went into hospital for her operation. Vicky had three-month-old Tom near enough full-time now. Stuart, her manager, now ran the office for her, and she worked from home and just went out to see clients when she had to. But she did a lot of work for Eric's company, so it was relatively easy to work at home.

Eric had been to the hospital with David that night. Dolly had had her operation and was stable. Vicky had cooked tea for them all and settled Tom down just in time for them to eat their tea. Afterwards, they sat in the living room and had a drink. "Vicky, I can't thank you enough for what you're doing for me with Tom, you know. You've been brilliant. I would have been lost without you," David said as he finished off his drink.

"Yes, well, we couldn't see you struggle and it's easy for me to work from home, and I love having him," she smiled at him.

"You too, big brother, thanks for all your help," he said to Eric as he got up.

"It's no problem' what's family for if not to help each other?" Eric replied. With that, David picked up Tom, said his goodbyes and walked home.

After clearing up, Vicky and Eric went up to bed. Eric came up behind her whilst she was getting undressed; he cupped her breasts with his hands and kissed her neck. "Have I ever told you just how much I love you?" he said as he muzzled her neck.

Vicky turned around in his arms and faced him, wrapping her arms round his neck. "Mm, just once or twice you have, but sometimes I need reminding," she said, kissing his lips.

"Well, I think I can manage that, Mrs Armstrong." And with that, they slowly and seductively undressed each other. Eric lifted Vicky onto the bed and they made love passionately, feeling the depth of each others' love.

Three weeks later Dolly came out of hospital. It was two weeks to Christmas and Vicky wanted to make it a special one for Tom's first Christmas and for Dolly, who had to take it easy. She arranged it all. David was spending Christmas with Vicky and Eric so he wouldn't be on his own on Christmas morning and everyone, including Vance, was coming for Christmas dinner.

"Have you got everything in that you need?" Dolly asked one afternoon when Vicky had driven over to see her with Tom.

"Yes, it's all in hand and it will be just fine, so stop worrying," Vicky said, smiling at her.

"Well, at least this year I get out of cooking the dinner," Dolly laughed.

"I can think of easier ways to do it though, can you?" Vicky laughed back.

Just then Tom woke up and started crying. "Hungry little bugger he is, it's only been an hour since he had his bottle," Dolly said, smiling down at him in his chair. Tom was now five months old and growing rapidly. "He's going to be a big one, just like his Dad and uncle Eric," she said, picking him up.

Eric stood six-foot-four in his socks and was built like a navvy, but he was Vicky's gentle giant and she loved him to bits. David wasn't much smaller at six-two and just as big. Just after Vicky got back home that same afternoon, the phone rang as she was sorting out Tom. She picked it up, expecting to hear Eric or David. "Hello, is that Vicky Armstrong?" a voice said.

"Yes, whom I talking to please."

"You don't know me, but I've been asked to pass on a message to you. It is that you're not to forget what's coming to you. Payback will be unexpected, okay." And with that, whoever it was put the phone down. Vicky stood there shaking. What on earth was she going to do? Two threats in a month; she would have to tell Eric but she couldn't bring herself to do so because she knew what he and David would do. Easiest thing to do would be to change the phone number, but how would she explain that? When Eric and David got back at tea time she had settled down a bit and tried to put it to the back of her mind.

"How's my girl been today," Eric said as he came in, put his arms around her as usual and kissed her, nearly hugging the breath out of her.

"Mm, I'm good now you are home," she said, looking up at him and kissing him.

Just then David came in too. He went straight over to Tom. "I can't believe how good you've got him, Vicky. Just look at him sitting there watching you two smooching."

Eric went over to David and put his arms round him. "You can have a smooch with me too if you want, brother," Eric laughed.

"Get off, you mad bugger," David said as he pushed him away, laughing too.

"Right, when you two have finished mucking about your dinner will be ten minutes," Vicky said as she smiled to herself. She loved it when they played up, and it really lifted her mood.

After dinner they went into the living room and had a drink. "Do you think Mom is going to be okay?" David asked, looking at Eric.

"Well, she seems like she is over the worst now, hopefully," Eric said as he got up to pour another drink.

"Yes, let's just hope so because it's really took it out of her. Don't pour me another one, mate, I've got to go and get this little one down," David said as he picked up Tom from his chair and said his goodbyes.

When David had gone Vicky and Eric settled down on the settee and watched TV. But Vicky couldn't concentrate properly. "Are you all right, sweetheart, you seem like you're on edge," Eric asked.

Vicky turned to face him. "I'm fine, I'm just tired," she lied. She hated lying to the man she loved, but what could she do?

"Come here and give me a hug," Eric said as he pulled her closer to him, kissing her. As usual, she just melted in his arms and before they knew it they were undressing each other. Eric was searching her body with his mouth, finding the places only he knew drove her crazy, and kissing them, making her even more eager for him. She arched her back, pressing herself into him, and he took her then and they were making love there on the sofa.

* * *

Christmas had arrived, and on Christmas Eve David moved in with Vicky and Eric until the new year. Even though he only lived a few doors away it made sense all round for him to do it, because of Tom. It was just easier. David and Eric went for a drink at the Thistle; they knew everyone in there now and got on really well with the manager, Mick, who they had done a lot of work for.

Vicky stayed at home with Tom. Ten o'clock came and she sat down on the settee with a glass of wine . Tom was fast asleep after having a feed half an hour ago. Vicky thought of Eric and how much she loved him, how much she loved how tall and broad he was, and he was so gentle with her. She loved every inch of him. Eleven o'clock came and just after that Eric and David ambled in, very merry indeed.

"Shush, you two, Tom's fast asleep," she said as she playfully hit them both.

"'K, okay," David said as he fell onto the settee, winking at Vicky. Eric went over to Vicky and playfully tickled her.

"You two had better get yourselves to bed," Vicky said as she laughed at being tickled. "Because if you fall to sleep here I'm not moving you, you big lumps; you can stop here," she told them as she tried to pull David up off the settee. She cleared away and tidied up. David let Vicky carry Tom upstairs in case he dropped him, and they all said goodnight and went into their rooms.

"Have you enjoyed yourself," Vicky asked Eric, laughing as he tried to unbutton his shirt.

"Yes, it's been great, it's just that these buttons have suddenly got a mind of their own," he said as he fell onto the bed, laughing. Vicky went over and started to undo his shirt. "Oh, so that's what your up to then is it, you're just after my body again," he laughed, pulling her onto the bed with him.

"I don't think you're in any fit state for that," she laughed as she tried to get up. Eric managed to get himself into bed with a lot of help off Vicky and then lay there, watching her get undressed. She got into bed and his arms were immediately round her and that's how they fell to sleep, spooned together.

Early Christmas morning Vicky was woken by Eric kissing her back, tracing her scars with his lips. "Morning, lover," she said sleepily, and he slid up the bed until he was leaning over her. She was on her stomach. He kissed her neck.

"You taste like heaven this morning," he whispered as he kissed her shoulders. He slid himself onto her and took her from behind, and she groaned with pleasure, pushing herself up to him.

They rolled onto their sides, never parting, Eric cupped her breasts with his hands and pushing her down onto him. "Jesus, Vicky," he whispered into her hair. She slid her arms up and round the back of his neck, holding him as their rhythm gained. They ached for each other, then the moment came and they exploded against each other. They lay there spooned together, regaining their breath, still not parting.

"I love you so much," Vicky whispered as he kissed her neck.

"I know, I love you too," he said, and he held her tight and they fell back to sleep.

"No Daddy, no, stop, it hurts, DADDY NO PLEASE!" Vicky shouted.

"Hey sweetheart, it's okay, I'm here," Eric said gently as he held her tight. Vicky had awakened with a start, crying as usual at the reality of her dream. She immediately turned and buried her head against his chest. Eric held her tight, not saying a word, letting her sobs subside. She hadn't had one of these for months now. Her sobs began to ease and she slowly raised her head and looked up at Eric. He could see the anguish in her eyes; it was always there after.

She reached up and kissed him gently on the lips and caressed his scarred face with her fingertips. "Thank you. I love you," she said and kissed him again.

"I know and I love you too," he said, and hugged her to him.

***

With Christmas over and New Year's Eve upon them, Vicky was busy. Vance had come back for New Year's Eve and had brought a great big hamper of food and drink with him. Everyone was staying at Eric and Vicky's that night, so the drink went around well. Dolly had to be careful so she kept an eye on Tom, who was now fast asleep. They saw the New Year in in style, and everyone was happy and jolly and the food went down a treat. They all went to bed about 3.30 am and left all the mess until morning.

When they were alone in their bedroom, Eric went up behind Vicky and just stood holding her for a few minutes. "I could hold you like this forever," he whispered in her ear, kissing her neck.

She turned around and kissed his scarred face. "Happy New Year, my handsome soul mate," Vicky said quietly as she gently kissed his lips.

Eric stood there looking down at her. He looked into her eyes and saw tears brimming in them. "What's wrong?" he asked.

"Nothing really, I just wish sometimes that I was able to give you the child you wanted. When I see you with Tom it brings it all back sometimes, that's all. And sometimes I think that you may go off me and find someone who can give you your child," she said as a tear trickled down her cheek.

"Oh Vicky, I never want to be with anyone apart from you. I love you more than life; all I want now is to get into bed with my beautiful sloppy wife and show her just how much I love her," he said as he started to undo her blouse. "Happy New Year, sweetheart," he whispered to her as he lifted her onto the bed and made her forget all her worries.

"I love you, Eric," she said as he caressed her.

"I know" was all he said, and then he was making love to her with the tenderness that she knew and loved.

***

January passed and all was well; everyone got on with their everyday lives. Eric was so busy at work that Vicky had started to miss him being home. One evening he finally arrived home about eight o'clock and was shattered, and all he wanted to do was shower and go to bed. Vicky couldn't believe it; he had never done that in the five years they had been married, but he did. The following morning he was up early and out of the house before she woke.

Lunchtime came and he didn't come home. It went on like that all week until Friday lunchtime came and she couldn't stand it any more, so she phoned him at work. "Eric, is that you?" she said as the phone was answered.

"Yes, what's up," he said.

"I was just wondering if you could get home earlier tonight. I want to see you," she said.

"You see me every night. Look, I'm going to have to go, we're run off our feet. See you later." And with that he was gone. She couldn't believe it. What had she done wrong?

At teatime David came as usual for Tom. "David, can I ask you something?" Vicky asked.

"Yes, anything. Fire away, what's up? I can see some thing's bothering you," he said as he put his arm around her shoulder.

"Do you know if there is something bothering Eric? It's just that he hasn't been himself and has hardly spent any time at home lately and I'm worried," she said.

David kissed the top of her head and it felt strange to her. "All I know is that he is really busy at work. He doesn't know what he's missing at home. You are every man's ideal wife, do you know that? Gorgeous, sexy, brainy and I love you for it," he said.

Vicky pulled herself away from him and looked up at him. "David, what are you saying?" she asked.

"Oh God, Vicky, don't take that the wrong way, I didn't mean it as it sounded, honestly," he said as he stepped back from her. They both burst out laughing.

"You had me worried then, you big daft thing," she laughed.

"No, don't worry, honest; as much as I would love to have a wife like you, I know just how much Eric loves you and you love him. But I will ask him why he is acting so strange."

Friday night, Eric came in late as usual. "Do you want any tea tonight, sweetheart?" Vicky asked as he made his way upstairs.

"No. I'm fine, thanks," he said, and went up into the bedroom.

This time Vicky followed him up; she had had enough. "Eric, what's wrong with you? Have I done something wrong? If so, will you tell me please?" she asked as he got undressed to get into the shower.

He stopped what he was doing and turned to look at her. "Why, what's the matter" he asked. It was then that he broke down and started crying.

Vicky was straight over to him and put her arms round him. "Whatever is wrong, please tell me, sweetheart," she whispered in his ear as she kissed him.

"Oh, I have been so stupid, Vicky. I thought I had lost you to David. You and he have grown so close lately. But he came to see me tonight and told me you had asked him what was wrong with me, that you were worried. We had a chat and he told me what he had said to you, and he told me just how stupid I was and I had to agree with him. I'm sorry for being such a pain, sweetheart, and for being so stupid. Can you forgive me for even thinking it?" he said as he looked down at her.

"Eric Armstrong, don't you know after all this time just how much I love you? You are my every breath; I never want to be without you ever," she said. And at that, he kissed her so longingly she couldn't resist. He undressed her and they were on the bed before they knew it, and they loved each other up more than they thought was possible. Afterwards they lay in each other's arms, told each other everything that had happened that week, and laughed about it. Later Eric went down and got them a glass of wine each. They sat in bed and drank it and talked some more; then they made love again longingly, and fell to sleep encased around each other.

***

March came round and life was good, or so Vicky thought. She received another letter. JUST TO REMIND YOU THAT YOU ARE NOT FORGOTTEN AND YOUR TIME IS GETTING NEAR. YOU WILL PAY FOR WHAT YOU DID AND SO WILL THAT FUCKER OF A HUSBAND OF YOURS, HE WILL BE

LEFT WITH NOTHING, NOT EVEN YOU. YOU'RE DEAD
MEAT, BITCH.

This time Vicky became really frightened. I have got to tell
Eric, she thought, he will go mad at me not saying straight away
but I need to tell him now, because it involves him too. She
found out the other letter and phoned him. "Eric, I need to see
you sometime now. Can you meet me in the park?" she asked.

"Yes, if you can give me half an hour. What's up, are you
okay?" he asked.

"Yes, I'm fine, don't worry. I'll see you about eleven then
in the park. I love you," she said. They finished off and she put
the phone down, picking it up immediately and phoning David.

Someone answered and she asked to speak to him. "Hello
Vicky," came David's voice down the phone. "Is everything
okay with Tom?" he asked.

"Yes, he's fine, don't worry. Can you meet me in the park
about eleven? I wouldn't ask if it wasn't important," she said.

"Er, yes, that will be okay. Are you sure every thing is all
right?"

"Yes, fine really. I'll see you there then, bye," and she put
the phone down. Inside, Vicky was terrified. She knew both Eric
and David were going to go mad at her, but she didn't care now.
She wrapped Tom up and put him in his pram, put the two letters
in her bag and went out. When she got there Eric and David were
there looking rather confused as to why the other one was there.

"Vicky, what's going on?" Eric said coming up to her and
kissing her.

"Is everything okay?" David asked.

"Please, let's find a bench and I will tell you," she said,
pushing the pram towards an empty bench away from the path.
They sat down and Vicky got the letters out of her bag. "Now,
before I show you these, I want you both to promise me you
won't go mad at me," she said looking at them both as they sat
down either side of her. She gave Eric the letters and sat there
while he read them and handed them to David.

"When did you get these?" Eric asked, turning to look at her.

"I had one this morning and I got the other one just before your mom went into hospital. But I had a phone call in between, too," and she told them about that.

Eric was up off the bench and pacing about. "Why the bloody hell haven't you told me about this before, Vicky. You know we don't have secrets; it's always been our thing, so why keep this fucking quiet," he ranted.

"Eric, calm down and try and see her point," David said, getting up and going over to him.

"I'm sorry, Eric, but I just tried to put it to the back of my mind, thinking it was nothing," she said, looking up at him with tears brimming in her eyes. Eric came back over to her and pulled her to him, wrapping his arms around her.

"That bloody tart of an ex-wife of mine has got some explaining to do, believe me," David said, looking down at the letters again.

"You can't say anything. What proof have we got that it's her, even though we know it is?" Vicky said.

"That's true," Eric said, holding onto Vicky.

"Well, now you have told us, you're not on your own and we will think of something, I don't know what exactly, but something, and if you get anything else you tell us, okay," David said as he handed the letters back to Vicky. Half an hour later they parted, Eric and David back to work and Vicky going home.

Later that afternoon when Eric came home, he sat in the kitchen and watched Vicky as she saw to Tom and started to prepare the tea. He loved this woman so much; if anyone ever hurt her he didn't know what he would do. "Please don't keep anything from me again, Vicky," he said softly, looking over at her.

She came over to him, sat on his lap and wrapped her arms around his neck, and kissed him tenderly. "I'm sorry, I won't ever again, I promise, but I didn't know what to do."

"I know, what's done is done now, but please Vicky, don't shut me out of things that involve you. I love you," he said and rested his head against hers, holding her tight. She hugged him to her, feeling safe.

"I love you too, more than anything."

Not long after, David was back and they sat and spoke again while they ate their tea. "I've told Dad," David said. "Because I think that he needs to know what's going on, but we're not to say anything to Mom because he doesn't want her worrying, okay?"

"Yes, that's fine, we don't want Mom worried either," Eric said.

"If you get any more letters, Dad said we're to go to the police," David said as he got up to Tom.

"That's for sure," Eric agreed. David went home not long after and Vicky and Eric curled up together on the settee and watched TV.

CHAPTER FIVE

Tom's first birthday was upon them and it was an excuse for a get together. They invited friends from work and the village, and had a water party in the back garden. The kids loved it, but Vicky was sure that the adults loved it more, especially Eric and David; they were worse than the kids. Dolly revelled in being fussed over, too. She still wasn't quite right, but she was okay. Tony made sure she got plenty of rest. He was retiring at the end of the month, to be at home with her more. David and Eric were going to be in charge of his business, and David had told Vicky he would get a child minder if the hours with Tom got too much for her with her work, as they would be working longer days while they looked for someone suitable to become manager.

The months passed and everything was fine. Tom was getting about on his feet, hanging onto the furniture; he was comical to watch. He was even starting to try and say a few words. His eyes hardly ever left Vicky when she was in the room, and he was a really good baby. He and Vicky were just like mother and son, not aunty and nephew, but nobody minded. At the beginning of September, Vicky drove over to Dolly and Tony's; they were having Tom for a few hours while Vicky went to see a new client.

She dropped him off and got on her way; she hadn't got far to go. When she got to the address she had been given, she parked up and knocked the door. The lady who answered the door knew nothing of her coming, and didn't need an accountant. Vicky apologised and said she must have the wrong address. She phoned Stuart at the office, but he assured her that it was the right address. She then phoned Eric.

"Hello sweetheart," he said as she spoke to him. She told him of the address mix-up and that she was coming home, and she would call in to see him at the yard before she went back; she may as well make use of a free afternoon.

"I love you," she said before she went.

"I love you too," Eric said, and then he was gone.

On the drive back, Vicky never noticed the van that was following her. She was going down a country lane when suddenly a car pulled out in front of her, making her swerve. She looked in her mirror to see the van behind her put their foot down and ram into the back of her, sending her crashing down a ditch and straight into a tree. The car and the van slowed down; the drivers looked and then drove off at speed. An hour went by before another car came down and noticed her car down the ditch. An ambulance and fire engine were called and they began the task of cutting Vicky's limp and broken bloody body out of the mangled wreck.

It had been nearly two hours now since Eric had spoken to Vicky and she still hadn't turned up at work like she said she would. He phoned his mom and dad but they hadn't heard anything off her since she phoned them earlier to say she was calling in to see him. He then phoned David to see if by any remote chance she had gone to see him, but he hadn't heard off her. Eric went home at 4.30 pm; he was now getting worried, as nobody had heard anything off her. David near enough followed him in; he had spoken to his mom and dad and they were going to hold on to Tom for a while.

"I'm really worried now," Eric said to David. "This isn't like Vicky at all; she has never just gone off anywhere," he said.

Just then there was a knock at the door. They both went and as Eric opened it he saw a policeman and woman, and his legs buckled beneath him. "Oh dear God, no," he heard himself saying.

"Are you Mr Eric Armstrong?" the policeman asked. Eric was holding onto the doorframe to steady himself.

"Yes he is," David answered. "I'm his brother David, has something happened to Vicky?"

"There has been a really bad accident and we need you to come to the hospital with us, as we presume it is your wife that was driving the car that crashed," he said looking at Eric.

"What do you mean, you presume?" David asked. Eric couldn't talk; he was just numb inside and out.

"We found a bag in the wreckage and we presume it was your wife' s. Will you please come to the hospital with us?" The policewoman spoke this time to Eric. "She is barely alive, Mr Armstrong, we need to go," she said.

Eric only heard the word alive and he came to a bit. They both got into the police car and it sped away. They got to the hospital and were taken to the intensive care unit, where a doctor came out to see them. "Mr Armstrong?" the doctor asked.

Eric looked at him. "Yes, that's me, how's my wife'" he asked, dreading the answer.

"She has been in a horrific accident and at the moment she is in theatre being operated on, because she has heavy internal bleeding and we must stop it as fast as we can. She has a broken wrist, six broken ribs, a punctured lung and head and face injuries," he said. Eric collapsed onto the seat.

"Jesus!" David said. "What are her chances, doctor?"

"Not too good at the moment; we need to stop the internal bleeding, but I have to tell you that you will have a long wait before we will know any more," he said.

"Thank you, doctor, we will only be out here if you need us," David said as he sat down by Eric.

The doctor went and they both just sat there in shock. Just then, two policemen came in. "Mr Armstrong?" one asked. They both looked up.

"I'm the one you want, this is my brother., Eric said.

"I'm Inspector Castle and this is PC Hall," he said as he shook both their hands.

"What happened? Do you know yet" Eric asked.

"Well, as far as we can tell at the moment, it looks like she swerved and ended up sideways down a ditch hitting a tree. Did your wife have any damage to the back of her car at all?"

"No, none whatsoever, why?" Eric asked.

"It's just that it looks like something went into the back of her car, but there was no other vehicle involved," Inspector Castle said. "We are looking into exactly what happened and will keep you informed," he said and turned to walk away.

Eric and David just looked at each other, each knowing what the other one was thinking. "I'll go and phone Mom and Dad; they will be worrying" David said. He came back a few minutes later with two cups of coffee. "I've phoned both works and told them what's what and phoned Stuart."

"Right, cheers," Eric said, not really caring. He sat there just thinking of all the things he and Vicky had done together over the years. They had been married for five and a half wonderful years, apart from losing their babies and his accident; they had been contented with each other and loved each other beyond belief. She couldn't leave him now; it was too unbearable to think of. He just let the tears run down his face. David put a comforting arm around his brother's shoulder and sat and cried with him. He too couldn't imagine life without Vicky, and he knew it would completely destroy his older brother.

It was now 9 pm and Vicky had just come out of theatre. She had been in there for three hours. The doctors were brilliant. They kept them informed of everything, and David in turn was keeping his mom and dad informed. They wouldn't come to the hospital because of Tom, and Dolly wasn't really up to it. The doctor came out to see them about 9.30 pm to tell them that they thought they had stemmed the bleeding, and Vicky would remain sedated for another three to four days so as to keep her still. Her lung and ribs had been seen to, and they had taken an X-ray of her head to make sure there wasn't any damage there. Her wrist had been set in plaster. The worst bit was that she was injured internally, because part of the dashboard had spliced through her when it shattered.

"When will I be able to see her?" Eric asked.

"We can let you see her now, but only for a couple of minutes," the doctor said.

"Follow me." Eric followed the doctor into a side room in intensive care, where he saw his gorgeous precious wife. He didn't recognise her, she was so badly damaged. "Just a few minutes," the doctor whispered and left him there.

Eric took hold of her good hand and kissed it. He kissed her wedding ring and prayed to God that she would pull through okay. He gently kissed her cheek before he left the room. "I love you, Vicky, with all my heart," he whispered to her.

Back out in the waiting area, David looked up at him. "God, she's in a mess," Eric told him, and broke down crying. David stood up and held his big brother and they cried together. The following morning David left Eric at the hospital and went to see their mom and dad, and get himself and Eric some clean clothes. He explained everything to them and asked if they would be okay with Tom. They said they would, as Sarah was coming over to take him out, to give their mom a break because she tired so easily nowadays.

"Don't worry about a thing; everything is sorted this end, son," Tony said. "Just look after your brother, because if anything happens to Vicky, God help us, it will kill him."

"I know it will," David said as he left. David got back to the hospital about 10 am. He went straight into Eric. who was just sitting staring at the floor. He looked awful. "Have they said any more?" David asked him.

"No, not yet, but I suppose no news is good news," Eric said as he looked up at David.

"I'm going to get us a coffee," David said, and went back out. He couldn't bear to see his brother in this state. "Please Vicky, don't leave us," David said to himself as he looked out of the window up to the sky, praying for her to mend.

That afternoon, the police were back to see Eric. "Mr Armstrong, we need to ask you some questions," Inspector Castle said as he sat down.

"Fine," Eric said as he turned to look at him. "What do you want to know?"

"We think that your wife's car could have been forced off the road," he said.

"What !" Eric said as he looked at David.

"Do you know anyone who has a grudge against your wife or anything?"

Eric and David looked at each other, then David spoke up first. "My ex-wife," he said. They went on between them to relay the story to the inspector, and Eric told David to get the letters from the house. David was back within fifteen minutes.

The inspector was still talking to Eric when the doctor came out just in time for David to hear what he said. "Mr Armstrong, I'm afraid that we're going to have to take your wife back down to theatre, she has started bleeding again and we don't know if we will be able to stop it this time," he said gravely.

Eric collapsed onto the chair, the colour completely drained from him. "Eric, come on, sit up," David was saying as he tried to sit him up properly. The doctor had gone, but not before telling David they would keep them informed every step of the way. The inspector took his leave after getting the letters off David, and said he would be in touch soon.

Two hours later, the doctor came back out. "What's going on, is she going to be okay?" Eric asked urgently.

"We have managed to stem the bleeding again and hopefully it will hold, but your wife is very badly damaged, Mr Armstrong, and is going to take a long time to mend if she pulls through. We will keep you informed of everything," he said as he turned to leave.

"Thank you," Eric said quietly.

"If this is down to bloody Cora and that fanny of a bloke Leo, I swear to God they will pay," David said angrily.

"No," Eric said quietly, "just let the police deal with them if it is. Vicky is going to need us both, and so is little Tom."

"Yes, well, it will be easier said than done, but I can see what you're saying. Come on, Vicky, pull through for us please," David said quietly. The night passed slowly. David phoned their mom and dad regularly to keep them informed. Sarah popped into the hospital with Tom to see his dad early on, but didn't stay because she was concerned about Dolly. After hearing the news of Vicky, she had taken a turn and the doctor had to be called in for her. It added stress upon stress for them all.

The following morning about 8 am the doctor came out to see Eric. He was groggy from having hardly any sleep, and when he spotted him coming feared the worst. "Mr Armstrong," the doctor said quietly. Eric sat up and looked at him. "Your wife has had a stable night; she is still critical but the bleeding has been stopped now for nearly ten hours, so it is looking hopeful but not definite. Would you like to come and see her for a few minutes?"

Eric was up off his seat in seconds, and so was David. "Come on, David, you have been here all night, you're coming in with me," Eric said.

"Are you sure?" David said.

"Yes, it is what Vicky would want." They followed the doctor into the little room, and he said he would be back in a few minutes.

"Jesus, Eric, I know you said she was in a mess but I didn't think she would be this bad," David said, shocked at what he saw. Vicky was lying there with tubes and drips all over her. Her right wrist was plastered to the elbow and her face was black and blue and swollen, with stitches in her head and a split lip as well. They could just imagine all the dressing she had on her underneath.

Eric picked up her left hand and kissed it again. "Come on, sweetheart, pull through for us, we're all here for you," he said quietly.

"I'll leave you for a minute," David said as he walked out with tears in his eyes.

"I love you, Vicky Armstrong, you have got to come back to me. Fight, please," Eric said, then very gently kissed her swollen cheek and left the room.

***

A week went by, but there was little change in Vicky's condition. She was in an induced coma so her body could start healing. She was beginning to respond to treatment, but very slowly. Eric was in a mess. David could see him crumbling and couldn't do anything to help him. The police were still investigating the crash. They were having a problem finding Cora and Leo, but they had a lead where they might be. Two days later and nearly ten days after the crash, Cora and Leo were arrested. They both denied anything to do with it, obviously, but their fingerprints were found on both letters that Vicky had received, and the paint on the back of Vicky's car matched that of Leo's van. It was found that Cora had pulled out to make Vicky swerve in the road, then sat and watched as Leo rammed her car into the tree and over into the ditch. Then they both drove off, leaving Vicky to die.

Cora told police that Vicky had to pay for humiliating her and slapping her, and Eric had to pay for throwing her out of the house. She hoped Vicky died a painful death and Eric would be left with nothing. The police couldn't believe anyone could be so cruel over such a trivial thing. They were both charged with attempted murder, and locked up awaiting trial. Eric and David couldn't believe what they were hearing when the police told them. Once Eric knew Vicky was stable, he paid a quick visit home to see his mom and dad. He and David relayed the story of Cora and Leo to them both, and they were gobsmacked that anyone could be so cold-hearted and hateful, especially to someone like Vicky who wouldn't hurt a fly.

Two hours later Eric returned to the hospital. The doctor came to see him. "Mr Armstrong, I have been waiting for you to come back; we have a bit of encouraging news for you," he said, smiling at him.

"Please say that she is going to be okay," Eric said desperately.

"Well, she is starting to respond to treatment and the bruising round her head is starting to go down," the doctor continued.

"Oh, thank God for that. Thank you. You have all been brilliant," Eric said as he shook the doctor's hand.

Later that afternoon, David returned to the hospital. Eric had phoned them to give them all the news but David wanted to come back and stay with Eric, for which Eric was truly grateful. "The doctor has said we can go and sit with her for a bit later," Eric told David when he came back with two cups of coffee.

"That's great news," David said as he sat down. That evening they both went and sat in the room with Vicky. She was beginning to look a bit better; the swelling was going down in her face, but all the other marks were still present. "How long do you reckon it will take her to get over this?" David said to Eric as they sat there.

"This will probably sound really selfish, but as long as I have got my Vicky back in one piece, she can take as long as she needs. I really thought I had lost her, and that would have finished me off too, you know," he said.

"Yes, I do know, and Dad said the same," David said, looking over at his brother. Another two weeks went by, but all the time Vicky was mending inside and out.

It was now nearly the end of October. Vicky had been in hospital for over a month, and all that time she had been in an induced coma to help her with the healing process. Eric could now stay in the room with Vicky all the time. The doctor came in to see him one afternoon and said "We are going to wean her off the coma drug and slowly bring her round in the morning. So hopefully, by tomorrow night you may be able to talk to her." The doctor smiled at him.

"That will be wonderful. I have missed hearing her voice. But at least, thanks to you, I will hear her voice again," he said with tears in his eyes.

David came back that night and Eric relayed to him what the doctor had said. David was as overjoyed as Eric. "I will tell them all when I go home, and I will be back in the morning to sit with you, okay?" David said, smiling at his brother.

"Thanks, David. You have been a saviour, you know." The following morning. the nurse came in about 9 am and started to take out Vicky's drip. Eric sat there watching, looking at his wife lovingly and willing her awake. He had missed her so much, he couldn't wait to hear her voice again just to know that she was here.

The day went slowly by. Eric and David sat talking to each other, as they both willed Vicky to wake up. They in turn sat talking to her as well, so she could hear familiar voices. Teatime came and went and Eric was getting despondent. David went out to get them some coffee. It was the only thing that was keeping them awake; they were both so tired. When he came back he handed Eric his coffee, and they sat and talked about Tom.

Suddenly they heard a crackled voice: "I hope you've looked after him properly."

"Vicky. Oh, sweetheart, you're back with us. God, have we missed you," Eric beamed as he bent and gently kissed her lips.

"What's happened to me? God, I hurt all over. The last thing I remember was a van pushing me off the road," she croaked.

David had gone to fetch the nurse, who promptly came in and welcomed Vicky back into the land of the living. She carried out some tests to check her eyesight and heartbeat and blood pressure, and told them not to tire her out as she needed her proper rest now.

After she had gone, David got up and kissed Vicky's cheek. "We're so glad to have you back with us; you had us all really worried," he said quietly to her. He then left to phone home, to tell them the news and give Eric a bit of time on his own.

"I have missed you so much," Eric said with tears in his eyes.

Vicky looked over at him and saw how haggard he looked. "How long have I been in here?" she asked.

"Just over a month," he said as he held her hand and kissed it. "God, I hurt," she said as she tried to shift herself.

"You have been to death's door sweetheart. I really thought I had lost you more than once. I love you more than I ever have, if that is at all possible," he said, looking at her.

Just then, the doctor came in to see her. "Hello, Vicky," he said. "How are you feeling?"

"Very sore and aching all over," she said, smiling at Eric.

"Well, we will have you moving around, I hope, within the next couple of days; you have just got to take it easy, though. Now, I have to look at your stitches on your side if you don't mind," he said.

"No wonder I hurt there. What happened?" she asked.

"When you crashed, the dashboard shattered and spliced through you, piercing your lung and breaking six ribs" he told her.

"So I'm going to look even more of a mess round my side then," she said, looking at Eric.

"Well ,we stitched you as good as we could, but you had to have fifty-eight stitches" he said as he started to take the dressing off. Eric couldn't believe the size of the gash in his wife's side. No wonder she had so much internal bleeding! "Ah, that's healing well; the nurse will come and put you some clean dressing on, and hopefully your plaster can come off your wrist at the end of the week too," he said, looking at her.

"Thank you," she said as he went out of the room.

Eric got up and gently kissed Vicky's lips. "I love you and your scar," he said, smiling at her.

"At least it matches the rest," she said.

Just then David came back in, followed by the nurse. He could see what was going on and went to leave. "No, stay David"

Vicky said, looking at Eric. "I don't mind you seeing it, but you will be the only two that ever will."

David was like Eric; he couldn't believe the size of the wound in her side. No wonder she nearly died! "We will be back in a minute, sweetheart," Eric said as he got up. "We will leave the nurse in peace to sort you out." He motioned to David to follow him, and he did. Outside the room, Eric turned to David. "No wonder she nearly died in here, what with the size of that wound and everything else," he said with tears in his eyes.

"That's exactly what I thought when I saw it too," David said, looking at him.

"Well, we have just got to get her back on her feet now," Eric said, getting himself back together. They went back in when the nurse came out. "Everything all right?" Eric asked as they went in.

"Yes, fine, I was just asking the nurse what they had done and she told me. I couldn't believe it," Vicky said, looking over at Eric. Soon after David went home, leaving Eric with Vicky. They sat and talked for a short while, then Vicky dozed back off to sleep. Eric went for a walk to get some air. He felt like he had had a lead weight lifted off his shoulders. He could smile again and, best of all, he could love his wife again, something he thought he had lost. He walked the whole circuit of the hospital and then went back in and got himself another cup of coffee. He walked up to Vicky's room and felt elated; all he wanted now was to take his wife home and look after her. But he knew he had a while yet for that to happen.

Another week passed and Vicky was making good progress. She got up every morning and moved herself as painlessly as she could to get mobile. She had been in hospital for just over two months. All she wanted now was to be home for Christmas, and that was just six weeks away. She missed seeing everybody regularly; even though they came to see her, it wasn't the same. She missed little Tom, though David brought him in to see her three times a week; he was too fidgety to stay longer than half an hour. But he loved seeing her too, and always had a smile for her when he went. Three weeks later, Vicky was told she could go home. Her wrist had all but healed, and her bruises faded. She couldn't wait. Eric came to pick her up Friday dinnertime. He brought her the biggest bunch of pure red roses she had ever seen; they were gorgeous. She was up and dressed in the clothes he brought her in the day before. They were a bit big now, because she had lost over a stone and a half in weight. When he walked into the room, her heart burst with love for this man who had been to hell and back. She put the roses on the bed and gingerly pulled him to her. "I love you," she whispered as he gently put his arms around her, so as not to hurt her.

They left the hospital just after lunch, when Vicky had had her last checks and got all her medicines. They slowly walked down to the car. Vicky was holding onto Eric's arm; she didn't want to go out in a wheelchair. Her legs were a little shaky but she had her big strong husband, her gentle giant at her side, and that was all she wanted. They got down to the car and once she was in and settled, Eric started the engine and they were off. He pulled into a lay by just before they got to his mom and dad's, and turned off the engine. He turned and looked at Vicky, who was looking at him, and he leaned over, cupped her chin with his hand and kissed her. The kiss was so tender, it was just what Vicky had missed.

She pulled back a little and looked breathlessly into Eric's deep blue eyes. "I love you so much," she whispered to him.

"I know, that's why you came back to me," he said, kissing her again. With that, he gently hugged her and started the engine, and they were on their way again. They got back to Tony and Dolly's and everyone was there. Eric fussed over her like anything.

Sarah came and sat by her on the settee. "Are you feeling a bit better now?" she asked as she squeezed Vicky's hand.

"Yes, much better now that I'm near enough home, and Eric has been golden, just like he always is. I love him so much, Sarah, I can't tell you," she said as she looked over at her husband.

"I know you do. If you hadn't have made it through all this, it would have destroyed him. I have never met two people who love each other like you two do," she said.

Just then, Eric came over to them. "Would either of you two like a cup of coffee?" he said as he winked at Vicky.

"No thanks, Eric," Sarah said as she got up. "But you can come and sit here with your wife, and give her some fuss." She smiled at him and gave him a peck on the cheek.

Eric took Vicky's hand and squeezed it. "You okay, sweetheart?"

"Yes, I'm just glad to be out of hospital, but I'll be even better when I can go home properly," she said, smiling up at him.

"Well, we will get Christmas over with and see how you are in the new year, it's only about four weeks and you could be home in your own house if you behave yourself." He smiled at her and she laughed. "God, it's so good to see you laugh. I love you, Vicky," he said quietly as he leaned over and kissed her.

Just then Tom came bounding over. He was now one and a half, and he was lovely. "Viddy, Viddy," he shouted as he wobbled over. That was what he called Vicky, and she loved it.

"Hey soldier, what you up to?" Eric said to him as he leant down and picked him up. "Don't climb on Viddy, she's got a poorly tummy," Eric told him as he tickled him.

Vicky gingerly leaned across and kissed his chubby cheek. She then kissed Eric. "I love you too, more than anything," she said as she sat back, wincing.

"Are you hurting?" Eric asked.

"Just aching a bit."

David came over to retrieve his son. "Hey you, don't get playing Viddy up, come on, come and see granddad," he said to Tom as he took him off Eric. Dolly came over then, and Eric got up so his mom could sit down. He pecked Vicky's cheek and went over to his dad and Tom.

"How are you, my angel?" Dolly asked as she sat down.

"I'm getting there slowly," Vicky said as she looked at her.

"Glad to hear it, because I have never seen Eric look so lost and vulnerable as he did when you were in hospital at death's door. We really thought we had lost you. You scared us all, and Eric wouldn't have coped with that at all, never. It would have crucified him if he had lost you." she said. "But I'm so glad to have you back," she said, and gave her a big gentle Dolly hug.

"How are you doing, anyway? Is everything working out all right now?" Vicky asked, as she hadn't seen Dolly properly for weeks.

"Yes, the doctor says I'm doing good and everything is checking out okay. So I will be near enough back to normal just after the New Year, hopefully," she beamed. She hated having to sit about and rely on other people, but the rest had done her good and Tony had told her she was to wait until the New Year to try and get back, else she would have him to answer to. Vicky went up to bed about 9 pm. She was shattered. Eric took her up and promised he would be up soon, but she told him not to. She said to go and have a drink with his dad. He did come back up about twenty minutes later. Vicky was laying down and reading. He sat on the bed and put his arms around her and she sat nestled into his chest. They didn't have to speak; they understood each other perfectly. All they wanted to do was hold each other.

She tilted her head back and looked up at him, and he bent and kissed her. She returned the kiss and gently reached her one arm up around the back of his neck. They kissed for a while, then just lay there with each other, loving the feeling of being next to each other once again. It wasn't a passionate night because it couldn't be, but they had a loving night just laying in each others' arms.

The following morning Eric woke to find Vicky gone. He then heard her in the en suite. He looked round the open door and found her looking in the mirror at the angry scar and stitches on her side. "Are you okay?" he said as he went over to her and carefully wrapped his arms around her.

"I suppose so," she smiled at him in the mirror. Her scar went from just below her left breast over her ribs to just past her belly button.

"Well, at least now when we're bored we can compare scars and stitch marks," he laughed.

She looked at him in the mirror and smiled at him. "Well, I suppose I'm the lucky one there, really, because nobody can see mine except you," she said as she turned and put her arms around his neck and kissed him.

"Do you feel like going down to breakfast yet?" he said, looking down at her.

"No, not really, I want to spend some time with you. I've missed you," she said as she put her head on his chest. They went back in the bedroom and got back into bed, Eric wrapping himself around her like a protective glove. "Can we lie here like this for the rest of the day?" Vicky said as she kissed his hand that was wrapped round her.

"We can do the next hour at least. I think someone may come looking for us then, don't you?"

"Stands a very good chance," she replied as she snuggled into him. They lay there in another comforting silence, just enjoying being by each other. A little while later, Eric pulled himself away gently. Vicky had fallen back to sleep, and he didn't want to disturb her. He dressed and went downstairs to where his mom and Sarah were just clearing away the breakfast things.

"Have I missed breakfast?" he sighed. "I'm starving.

"There's tea in the pot. I'll do you some bacon and eggs if you want," Sarah said.

"No, it's okay, thanks. I'll just have tea and toast, and I'll take Vicky a tea up too."

"How is she this morning?" Dolly asked, sipping her tea.

He told them about finding her looking at her scar. "We got back into bed and I just lay there holding her until she fell back to sleep, that's why I'm a bit late down," he said, drinking his tea.

"There wasn't a specific time on breakfast, so don't worry," his mom said as she got up and kissed the top of his head as she passed him.

"I didn't really want to leave her alone like that, she's had a lot to cope with body wise, really," he said, going off in thought.

Just then he heard Tom shouting and chuckling, "Viddy, Viddy" and Vicky walked into the kitchen followed by Tom and David. "Look who I found coming down the stairs," David smiled as he picked Tom up to stop him jumping on Vicky as she sat down.

"Morning, everyone," she said as she looked round. Eric looked at her knowing something was wrong; she looked like she had been crying.

He got up and poured her a cup of tea. As he gave it to her, he whispered, "Are you feeling okay?" and sat down next to her at the table.

She turned her head and looked at him and nodded, but he knew her better and also knew she wouldn't say anything here. Sarah looked across the table and saw the exchanged look between the two of them. "Come on, little un, Aunty Sarah will get you washed and dressed and take you down the garden to feed the fish," she said as she picked up Tom and hugged him at the same time, giving David the nod to follow her. On her way out the kitchen she called Dolly out.

"What's up?" David asked as they stood in the hall.

"I think Vicky is upset about something, so I thought we could give them some time to themselves. Come on, you can come and give me a hand with him," she said, looking down at Tom wriggling in her arms.

"Yes, I did notice that. I will go and tell your dad to stay out the way too," Dolly said as she went up the stairs.

Back in the kitchen Eric was sitting looking at Vicky, and he could see the anguish in her face. She turned and looked at him, and the tears spilled down her cheeks. "Sweetheart, whatever's wrong?" he said as he pulled her to him. She sobbed against him and he just sat and held her until the sobs subsided a little. She pulled away and looked up at him. "Vicky, what's wrong, are you in pain or has something happened?" he asked, concerned.

"No, nothing like that," she whispered.

"What's wrong, then? Please tell me."

She looked into his eyes. "I can't give you children, I've got a body that resembles a map and I'm scared to death of losing you to someone better who has got it all. I know it sounds stupid, but I can't help it. I nearly died. At least if I had, you wouldn't have to look at my ugly body every night, or put up with me moping about and unable to do hardly anything for myself," she said looking at him.

"Vicky Armstrong, don't you even begin to think along those lines. I love you for you, for who you are and for the love you give to me. And if you had died, my heart would have died with you. You will get better and get back to normal, and we will start to live our normal lives again. I want you, and nobody will ever compare to you ever, and I love your body, I always have, as you can tell," he said as he held her close. She hugged him so tight she winced with the pain. He pulled away quickly. "Hey," he said, laughing. "Don't hurt yourself, I'm not going anywhere ever. I promise. I love you too much." And with that, he kissed her longingly. "And anyway, you have to look at my ugly face every day," he laughed, and kissed her nose.

"Oh Eric, how did I know you would put it all into perspective and cheer me up no end? That's why I love you so much," she smiled up at him. They left the kitchen and slowly walked out into the garden. Vicky couldn't walk too well at the moment because of her stitches and her aching bones, but she held Eric's arm and was fine. They walked down to Sarah and David, who were pushing Tom on the swing.

"You two okay?" David asked.

"Yes, we're fine, and thanks for giving us some space in there; Vicky was feeling a bit low," Eric said as he gave Tom's swing a push.

"Bit chilly out here this morning, you're not to stay out here too long," Sarah said to Vicky as she held her arm.

"No, actually I think I might go in now; it is a bit cold and I would love a cup of tea," she said.

"Come on, then; we'll leave the men out here," Sarah said, and turned towards the house with Vicky on her arm.

Eric and David stood talking for a bit while they both played with Tom. "How would you like to come into partnership with me?" Eric asked David.

"What, me and you? What sort of business would we have together?" David asked, surprised.

"Well, how about the Golden Thistle?" Eric answered.

"What, buy the pub in the village and us two run it?" he asked, laughing.

"Yes, well, there's a method in my madness, actually. It's got a great living quarters upstairs, four bedrooms, two bathrooms, et cetera, and I had the idea of moving Mom and Dad there if they wanted. Get a manager in, or whatever. Give Dad something to do, and if Mom felt up to it she could do a bit of cooking and whatnot. It would also mean that we would all be close together, too. Me and Vicky and you and Tom are just down the road. And so is Sarah. It would be great," Eric said, smiling.

"You've really thought this through already, haven't you. What does Vicky think?" David asked.

"I haven't had a chance to ask her yet, what with everything else. I had the idea before her accident, so it hasn't got any further yet apart from talking to Mick. Don't say anything yet, because I want Vicky to know first; will you think about it?" Eric said, looking back at the house.

"Yes, I surely will; it sounds like a great idea," David said as he took Tom off the swing. "Come on, trouble, it's getting cold out here," he said to Tom, who was wriggling about in his arms. They walked back up to the house, both of them deep in thought. They walked into the kitchen to find the three women discussing clothes and drinking tea as usual. Tony was by the fire reading his paper. Eric went up to his mom and gave her a hug.

"Come on, then, what have you done, beings as I have had a hug for nothing," she laughed.

Vicky looked up at him and he was smirking. "I haven't done anything yet," he said, and winked at David.

"That sounds ominous," Tony said, looking up from his paper. Vicky could tell he was up to something; she knew him like the back of her hand.

"What are you two plotting now?" Dolly asked as she found Tom a biscuit and some toys.

"That's for us to know and you to find out later," Eric said, smiling and winking at Vicky.

"Well, for now you can all clear off out of my kitchen so we can get dinner sorted, and you, young lady," she said to Vicky, "can go and have a lie down."

Vicky didn't argue. She was feeling a bit drained. She got up, and Eric held her arm and took her upstairs. When they were in their room, she asked him, "What are you up to now?"

"Nothing yet, but when you have had a rest I want to ask you something, and I'm not saying any more until you have," he said as she got into bed. He sat on the bed with her and held her, and she cuddled up to him.

"You are wonderful, do you know that?" she said to him, and her eyes began to close.

"Yes, and it's because I love you so much," he whispered as she fell to sleep in his arms.

A couple of hours later Vicky woke to find herself tucked up in bed. Eric had laid her down and covered her over. She carefully sat herself up and looked round the room. She loved it here; she always had, since she was little. It was a house filled with love and laughter; even though they hadn't had much laughter lately, there was plenty of love. She got up and got herself washed and dressed, gingerly moving around the room as she still hurt quite a bit. She sat on the edge of the bed just as Eric came in.

"Hey, you're up and about. I was just coming to see if you were awake. You feeling a bit more with it now you've had a rest?" he said as he sat next to her on the bed.

"I feel much better now, in fact I feel quite well apart from aching; that rest has done me the world of good and seeing you has made me feel even better," she said as she leaned over and kissed him.

"Dinner's nearly ready, if you feel up to coming down and eating," he said as he responded to her kiss.

"I will come down and have some dinner. I feel quite hungry actually, but are you going to tell me what you're up to now? I've done as I was told and had a rest," she smiled at him.

"When you have eaten something and you're fully alert, I promise you that we will go for a drive out and I will tell you everything, okay," he said as he helped her up and kissed her nose, laughing.

"I haven't got a lot of choice there then, have I?" she smiled as they made their way downstairs. Once dinner was over and everyone was settled into the living room, Eric got Vicky's warm coat and they went out for a drive. He pulled up into a park and they sat looking across a lake; it was lovely.

"Right. I don't want you to say a word until I have finished, okay," he said, turning to her and holding her hand.

"Okay," she smiled. He told her all about the pub and what he had asked David, and the ideas that he had for it all. He would have a business loan to pay off Mick and do the renovations needed, but there was a good business there. He looked at Vicky, hoping that she would like the idea, but she never said a word. "Vicky, what do you think then," he asked, urging her to say something.

She looked into his eyes and smiled. "I think it's a wonderful idea, but you won't have a business loan, you pay too much back," she said.

"But without it we will be short to pay Mick and do the renovations," he said, deflated.

She sat there looking at this wonderful man who she loved beyond reason. "Well, no business loan," she smiled at him.

"What's so funny," he asked, smiling back at her.

"You don't need a loan, sweetheart."

"But how else would we do it?" he asked, puzzled.

"I will put 'his' money into it, it's just sitting there waiting for a rainy day, and today it's raining. I think this is the perfect thing for it," she smiled up at him.

He leaned over and gave her the kiss of all kisses. "Vicky Armstrong, you are absolutely wonderful, do you know that, and I love you more than ever., he said as he kissed her again. "Are you sure about 'his' money, you don't have to," he said.

"There is plenty there for us not to worry about a thing, because I have never touched it," Vicky told him.

"What, never?" he asked.

"No. Not since the day it went into the bank. But there is a substantial amount there, as you know. We have never needed it, so it's just been sitting there for a rainy day, and like I said, today it's raining," she laughed. They kissed tenderly and then just sat, looking across the lake.

When they drove back home, Vicky felt as if everything was coming up roses. She had her business, which was doing well thanks to having so much work off Eric's property business. She had a loving family, a bonny little nephew who was like the son she could never have, a beautiful home, and she was getting better by the day. But most of all, she had a husband she loved passionately, and he her. Everything was great. They got back just before teatime.

Before they went into the house Eric stopped her outside, put his strong arms around her and kissed her again. "Thank you," he said quietly, looking down at her.

"What for?" she asked.

"For coming back to me, for getting better and for believing in me. I love you, Vicky," he said.

She responded to his kiss with longing. That night they sat down with David, who had told them that he would do it, and told Tony and Dolly their plans. "It sounds good," Tony said. "But it will be a lot of upheaval for us." he continued.

"Everything will be sorted properly and you needn't lift a finger if you don't want to," Eric told them.

"What about my garden, though?" Dolly said.

"We will sort you part of the pub garden and do it up just for you just how you want it," Vicky told her.

Eric just looked at Vicky, amazed. "That will cost a bit, though," Tony said.

"That's no problem, don't you worry about that. Why don't you rent this out to start with, just in case you don't like it, and then you have the choice to come back if you want," Vicky said, looking at Eric and David, who were sitting gobsmacked listening to her. "We will even do out the kitchen in the flat to your very own design if you want," Vicky continued. Eric was looking at her with admiration. What a woman his wife was. No wonder he loved her like he did. "Everything you want re-designed we will do for you, because you have been like a proper mom and dad to me over the years and I want to do this for you," Vicky said, looking at them and smiling.

When they went up to bed later, Eric gently pulled Vicky to him when they got in their room. "I hope we can afford to do all that you told Mom earlier," he said quietly.

"I know we can," she smiled up at him. "I just haven't had the chance to tell you yet because we haven't had any time on our own really," she said.

"And what's that?" he asked.

"Well, I think you had better sit down first, because I know I need to," she said, moving over to the bed. Eric sat beside her. "When I phoned the bank earlier to have my account updated they told me the new balance, because I haven't done it for years or looked at it, I've just left it and forgotten about it." She smiled and kissed him. "They told me the balance is £925.000. I nearly fell through the floor."

"Bloody hell, Vicky, that's brilliant for you," Eric beamed.

"No, it's brilliant for us, because I have transferred £500.000 of it into our joint account for us to use on our new project."

Eric looked at her, stunned. "You mean we can go ahead straight away now?" he asked.

"Yes, we have enough money up front for everything and anything we want, with some left over."

Eric hugged her. "God, I love you so much. I could love you long and hard at the moment, but I know I can't yet and it doesn't matter. You're here," he said, kissing her face all over.

"I wish you would because I'm longing for you something terrible, I need you," she said, kissing him back. They lay back on the bed and Eric gently undressed her while she looked up at him, her body yearning for him. It had been over three months since they were last able to make love, and she wanted him more than ever.

Eric looked down at her with the same yearning. He bent and kissed her breasts and her stomach. He very gently kissed her healing scar. "I want you so much, Vicky."

"I want you too, now," she whispered. With that, she pulled off his shirt as best she could and he pulled off his trousers. He was hard for her beyond belief. He carefully lowered himself onto her, minding her side, and entered her gently, and she gasped with delight as they clung to each other. They made love passionately, carefully and gently because it had been so long. After they lay holding each other, entwined together, knowing another chapter of their lives was just beginning.

CHAPTER SIX

It was now May 1993. Eric and Vicky were coming up to their eighth wedding anniversary. The Golden Thistle was doing well, and everything was great. They had been there nearly two years now, and they got on really well with all the locals. "Shall we throw a party?" Eric said to Vicky one Saturday lunch time when they were having a bit of time to themselves in their house.

"That would be fun," Vicky said to him as she kissed him. Their love for one another was still as strong as it had ever been, if not stronger. David was yet to meet someone else he could fully trust again, but he spent the majority of his time with Vicky and Eric, as he was a partner in the pub. Little Tom was now coming up to four years old, and was at nursery. Tony and Dolly now managed the pub and loved it, and all the regulars loved them.

"Well, actually we could have two parties. An adult one for us, and next month we can throw a kiddies' party for Tom," Vicky said as she got up off the settee.

"That's a good idea, we can invite some of the moms and you never know, David might meet someone," Eric said as he playfully pulled her back down to him. "Come here, you," he said as he kissed her and started undoing her blouse. "After all these years together, you still turn me on just looking at you," and he worked his way to her breasts and kissed them too.

"Mm, you can do that all day if you want," Vicky said as she groaned with pleasure. "I love you, Eric Armstrong," she whispered as she undid his trousers and aroused him even further. He worked his way down her body, kissing it and stroking it where it mattered. He kissed her scar, which was now just a red line across her stomach, and then came back up and kissed her passionately on the lips. She in turn let her hands wander all over him, playing the teasing game. He rolled off the settee onto the floor, pulling her on top of him, and they were engrossed with each other, stripping off each others' clothes. In no time he was on top of her, and they were making mad passionate love in the middle of the living room. When they had got their breath back and were dressed again, they walked down to the Thistle hand in hand for a drink.

"Well, hello you two, we didn't expect to see you this afternoon," Tony said as they walked in.

"We thought we would come and see everyone when we didn't have to work for a change, stand the other side of the bar," Eric said as he got them both a drink from behind the bar.

"How's things, it's looking busy," Vicky said as she took her drink off Eric and sat down on a barstool at the end of the bar.

"We have had a really busy lunchtime today, lots of tourists coming through and that new guest house up the road helps too," Dolly said, coming over. Just after Christmas, a new guest house called Ivy Cottage had opened at the near end of the village, and was doing very well. Vicky had managed to get to know Maria, the owner. She was a divorcee, and very nice, and worked hard. She and Vicky had come to an agreement that they would recommend each other to punters, and it worked well.

"Talking of guest houses, we've got to invite Maria to our party, she and David would suit each other just nice," Vicky whispered to Eric, who sat on the stool next to her just as David walked over.

Eric turned and kissed her. "Sneaky, stop matchmaking," he laughed.

"Afternoon, you two, what brings you out on your day off?" David said as he came over and kissed Vicky on the cheek.

"We were missing you," Eric laughed.

Just then, Maria came in. "Hello Maria, it's unusual to see you in here on a lunch time," Vicky said to her as she walked over to them.

"I was bored, and this is the only pub I will walk into on my own because I know your mom and dad and you three," she said as she ordered a drink.

Eric nudged David and nodded his head over to Maria. "Don't go there," David whispered to him, and nudged him back.

"Coward," Eric laughed. They sat and had a few laughs with some of the locals, then the quiet period came before the evening started. Saturday nights they had three bar staff on, all local to the village; this gave all of them a night off together. Tonight Dolly and Tony were staying upstairs for a rest. Eric told David he would meet him for a pint about 9 pm so they could see how things were going. They liked to keep an eye open on a Saturday night in case of any drunks, which had been known. They left there about 4 pm and walked home. David walked back with them as far as his house; Sarah was dropping Tom back in half an hour. They arranged to meet later, and Eric and Vicky walked home.

"Don't you think Maria is nice?" Vicky said to Eric as she kicked off her shoes.

"Yes, she is okay, actually," he said, pulling her to him again. "But there again, nobody compares to you in my eyes, so I'm biased," he said as he kissed her.

Vicky kissed him back, then held his hand and led him up the stairs. In the bedroom she undressed him seductively, and in turn he started undressing her. She pushed him onto the bed and straddled across him. He reached up and pulled her to him, kissing her and caressing her breasts. She sat upon him, and he entered her with lust. His hands were reaching up all over her body, as he watched her and loved her with fury. They rolled over and caressed each others' bodies, exploring everywhere and everything. The height of their passion was nearing and he was upon her, entering her again and they reached to their souls together, collapsing against each other in contentment. They lay there for a while in silence; just being together was enough that they didn't have to talk.

The phone rang and woke them. They had fallen to sleep wrapped in each other, and it was now 7 pm. "Eric, it's David, got a bit of a problem. One of the bar staff has phoned in sick, I can't cover tonight because of Tom and I don't want to ask Mom to have him; she needs a rest and Sarah is already having him for another couple of hours or so later. Any chance you or Vicky can cover?" he said down the phone.

"Yes, don't worry, we'll be down there in a half hour, will you let them know? I'll just shower and get dressed," Eric replied as he looked at Vicky, just waking up.

"What's up?" she asked sleepily.

He leaned over and kissed her. "Staff, that's what's up, or should I say lack of them," he said as he got up.

Vicky grabbed his hand. "Come back to bed for a few minutes," she said as she rolled over, exposing her breasts from under the sheet. He looked down at her, tempted by what he saw. She could see he was aroused already, and he caved in and got back into bed with her and they made love again before he left for the pub.

Nine o'clock came, and in walked David. Eric was behind the bar and Vicky was sitting on the barstool at the end. David went up and kissed her cheek as usual. Eric came over with a drink for him and a fresh one for Vicky, winking at her as he put them on the bar. She and David sat and talked business for a while; the pub was busy. About an hour before closing, a group of youngish men came in. They were on a stag night and were a bit rowdy. They came up to the bar and ordered their drinks.

One of them kept staring at Vicky. "Hello gorgeous, all alone are we,"

Eric didn't need to step in because David was just behind her with his back to her, talking to one of the locals. He heard him and just turned and looked and knew Vicky was okay. One of the men came over to Vicky and started talking to her. He was a bit tipsy but nothing to worry about, not that Vicky worried because on either side of the bar were two men built like navvies, her husband and his brother.

"Well, fancy meeting someone as gorgeous as you here sitting all alone," he said to her. "I'm Mark, by the way."

"Pleased to meet you, Mark. Are you enjoying yourself?" Vicky answered, looking across at Eric and smiling. They always made people feel welcome.

"I will now I have met you," he answered, looking round at his mates. Eric came over to take his order. "Pint of lager, mate, please," Mark said. Eric went to pour his drink, looking at Vicky and giving her a cheeky grin. "Blimey, you seen the face on that, bloody mess. Pity the poor sod who has to wake up and see that every morning, scare you to death," he laughed.

Straight away, Vicky's back was up. How dare he insult her Eric like that! But she was used to people saying things. "Mm," was the only answer she gave. Eric came and gave him his drink and then stood by Vicky. David came back then and started talking to Eric.

"Wouldn't want to meet them two up a dark alley," Mark said to Vicky, looking at Eric and David.

She laughed. "No, you wouldn't." Eric was about to clock off, leaving the other two bar staff to finish off. He came round the other side of the bar to Vicky, kissed her and sat down on a stool. She now had David behind her and Eric at her side.

"Do you know these two giants, then," Mark asked.

David and Eric looked at each other, fit to burst out laughing. "Yes I do actually, this is my brother-in-law David, and this is my husband Eric, and we own the pub," she said smiling at him.

"Oh, bloody hell. I dropped myself in it there then, didn't I," he said, smiling at her. "I'm sorry" he said.

David put his hand on Mark's shoulder and he nearly jumped out of his skin. "Don't worry, mate, it's just a bit of harmless fun we have," David said to him.

"Would you like a drink on the house?" Eric asked him.

"Yes, cheers." Eric went and got them all a drink, and they sat talking. It worked out that Mark was the one getting married next week. Vicky chastised him for flirting like he did, and he then invited them to his wedding.

"How long have you two been married then, not long I wouldn't imagine, the way you are with each other, you're like a couple of newlyweds," Mark asked.

"Eight years, actually," Eric said proudly and put his arm round Vicky, who promptly kissed his scarred cheek.

"Blimey, usually by then you just tolerate each other, what's the secret?" he asked.

"Don't ask," David answered, smiling at Eric. They finished their drinks off and Mark disappeared with his mates, telling them to make sure they came next week. When they had all finished helping to clear up, the bar staff went home and the three of them had a last drink.

"He seemed like a really nice bloke," David said as he downed his drink.

"Yes he did," Vicky replied.

"You want to go next week?" Eric asked the pair of them.

They all looked at each other and laughed. "Why not?" Vicky said. They locked up and went home. David went into his house and Vicky and Eric carried on home.

When they got in, Eric turned to Vicky and hugged her. "I love you, Vicky Armstrong. And I always will. You mean the world to me and I will always try to make you happy. You know that, don't you?" he said as he kissed her tenderly on her lips.

She looked up at him lovingly and stroked his face with her fingers. "I love you too, more than anything, and you have always made me happy," she whispered as she reached up and kissed him too. The love they shared was unbelievable. Even David got jealous of them sometimes but not nastily; he loved them both for it. They were never far apart and they always made a point of telling each other everything. David once told

Eric that that was why they knitted together so well, because they had no secrets from each other and respected each other. Something hard to find in another person. Eric did no more than pick her up and carry her upstairs, telling her just how much he loved her again and vowing to show her once they were in their room.

"Why have we got to wait until we are in our room?" Vicky said huskily.

Eric stopped and put her down on the halfway landing, and kissed her hard. She started undoing his shirt whilst he started undressing her. Their clothes tumbled down the stairs. Vicky put her arms around his neck and wrapped her legs around his waist. Eric held on to her, turned and put her back up the wall. He entered her there and then on the landing against the wall, and they had the most wonderful uninhibited sex.

The following morning Eric got up to make some tea. As he went down the stairs he saw the clothes there and smiled to himself, thinking about the night before. He was so lucky to have a wife like Vicky; her love for him was as passionate as his for her. He had heard many a man at work saying that their wives had given up the ghost in the bedroom department. He made the tea and went back upstairs, smiling again as he passed the clothes. He would pick them up later. He entered the bedroom and looked at Vicky, who was asleep on top of the bed, naked. He was already aroused from thinking about the night before; this just completed it for him. He knelt on the bed and started kissing her breasts, making his way down to her stomach. His hands were exploring her body. He felt her hands slide down his back.

"Mm, good morning, sexy" she groaned. Her hands glided over him like silk. He was so aroused for her. He slid on top of her and they made passionate love, teasing each other for the next two hours, the tea forgotten.

***

The week went by with all the usual things going on. Mark stuck to his word and sent an invitation for the three of them to come to his wedding. He had told them about Dee, whom he was marrying, and she sounded quite nice. Saturday arrived and the three of them went to the next village for his wedding. The church was lovely and Dee, Mark's wife, looked lovely too. They sat at the back as they didn't know anyone, but once outside after the service Mark came over to them and introduced Dee. "I'm glad you came," he said. "Don't get disappearing too, early, enjoy yourselves" he said, shaking Eric and David's hands and pecking Vicky's cheek.

"I love your dress," Dee said to Vicky, who was wearing a coral-coloured fitted dress with a sweetheart neckline with mock buttons; it suited her with her dark hair.

"Thank you, but it should be me telling you that you look good today, which by the way you do," Vicky said as Eric came over and took her hand.

Dee was staring at him, and it made Eric feel uncomfortable. "Mark has told us that you're moving into the old mill cottage in Little Haven," Vicky said.

"Yes, straight after our honeymoon next week," Dee replied. She kept sneaking glances at Eric, and he didn't like it.

"We will be neighbours then, because we all live there and own the pub," Vicky said as Eric put his arm round her.

"That's great, we will have to get together," Dee said as she walked over to some other guests, still looking at Eric.

"Are you okay, Eric," Vicky asked, looking at him.

"Yes, it's just that she makes me feel uncomfortable for some reason," he said as he squeezed her waist. David came over then.

"Dee makes Eric feel uncomfortable. But I can understand why," Vicky said.

"I know, I did notice her staring at you, she is a bit strange though, isn't she?" David said to Eric.

"Just a bit," he replied.

The following week Mark and Dee moved into their cottage. On Saturday night they came in the pub for a drink. Vicky and

Eric were at the end of the bar; David was working with his dad serving. "Hello," Dee said as they came over to them.

"Have you settled in okay?" Vicky asked, looking at them both.

"Yes, getting there slowly," Mark said as he ordered some drinks. Straight away, Eric could feel Dee's eyes on him.

"Would you like to come to dinner next week?" Dee asked as she took her drink. Vicky heard Eric sort of grunt, and she had to grin and look away.

"Yes, that would be great if you could," Mark added.

"We will check our work rota and let you know," Vicky said as she put her arm through Eric's.

They stood there for a bit longer, then Mark went and found them both a seat. "We will love you and leave you, then. Don't forget to let us know about dinner," he said as they walked away.

"We will," Eric said, smiling falsely as they went.

"Eric Armstrong, I have never heard anything so false in all my life," Vicky said, laughing, and kissed his cheek.

"Yes, well, I've come to the conclusion I don't like her. He's okay. But her.!" he said.

"She is a bit full on, isn't she," Vicky agreed, looking over at them and noticing how Dee stared at Eric. They didn't manage to get out of dinner; they thought if they got it over with this once they wouldn't have to go again. Friday night, the night before their wedding anniversary party which they had had to invite them to, they went round to their house. Dee had cooked a lovely meal and they made them feel really welcome. But Eric couldn't shift this feeling of discomfort. He kept close to Vicky all night as Dee kept trying to sit between them, something Vicky noticed too. They left about eleven saying goodnight at the door. Dee made a beeline for Eric to kiss him goodnight, but he saw her coming and took Vicky's hand and walked down the path waving goodnight.

"God, am I glad to be out of there," Eric said to Vicky as he put his arm around her.

"Yes, me too really, it was rather heavy, wasn't it," she said as she got the house keys out of her bag. They got in the house, and Eric went and poured them both a drink. He handed it to her as she sat on the settee and he sat down beside her.

"I don't want to do that again; we will think of any excuse there is, but we're not doing it again," Eric said as he pulled Vicky against him.

She looked up at him. He really was uncomfortable about Dee, but there again Vicky was starting to feel the same. The following night was their party. The function room in the pub had been decorated with banners and balloons, and all was ready. Back home, Eric and Vicky were about to get ready to go.

"I'm going up to have a shower," Vicky said as she got up off the settee and kissed him.

"Okay, I'll be up in a minute," Eric said as he watched her. He waited for her to get up the stairs and listened for the shower to go on, then went up after her. He got himself undressed and then went into the bathroom. He went up behind her in the shower, put his arms round her and started kissing her shoulders. She immediately responded to him, turning in his arms and put her arms around his neck. "Sneaky," she said to him smiling. They kissed, and then she wrapped her legs around his waist while he held her. With her back against the shower wall, he told her he loved her and entered her lovingly and they made love there in the shower, not being able to get enough of each other amidst the cascade of water.

They were getting dressed when the phone rang. "Hello Eric, it's David. Mom said can you bring Dad's cuff links with you, please."

"Yes, fine, I forgot I'd got them actually," he replied.

"Okay, see you in about twenty minutes then," and with that he rang off.

"You look gorgeous," Eric said to Vicky as he turned round and saw her in her new black dress. It had a fitted bodice with off-the-shoulder lace sleeves, a plunge neckline, and it came just above her knees. "It's going to be another one of those nights isn't it," he said to her, grinning.

"What do you mean?" she said, smiling over at him.

"You know exactly what I mean, Mrs Armstrong. One of those nights when I've got to look at you looking like that all night. It's going to drive me crazy."

"Yes, well, let's hope it does," she said teasingly, and went over to him and kissed his cheek, and he growled at her lovingly as he squeezed her waist. They walked down to the pub ten minutes later and as they entered, everyone was there. David came up to them with two glasses of champagne and kissed Vicky.

"Happy anniversary," he said to them.

"Thanks," they said together. They went round and mingled with their guests while the music played. Then Vicky happened to look up to see Dee making her way over to Eric, who was walking over to his dad. Dee stopped him halfway, and reached up and kissed his cheek. Eric tried to back away but she was holding his arm, and he grimaced. She then whispered something to him, and the look on his face was shock. He then said something back to her and she walked off looking back at him, tapping the side of her nose and winking. He just stood there shaking his head when he saw Vicky coming over to him.

"All right, sweetheart?" she asked him.

"Yes, apart from that bloody woman," he said, looking over to Dee.

"What's she done now, then?" Vicky asked.

"She only said to me that she will see me round the back and show me what a woman is made of. Cheeky cow, as if she's got a patch on you.."

Vicky was shocked. "Oh, Eric, that's disgraceful. I don't like her at all, do you?" she said.

"No, I bloody well don't, not when I've only got eyes for you. No one compares to you," he said as he put his arms around her.

"Well, take no notice of her then, she will have me to answer to if she carries on anyway," Vicky said as they walked over to his dad, who was talking to Vance.

"Hello, angel," Vance said as he kissed her cheek.

She hugged him. "Where have you been hiding? We haven't seen you for ages."

"I've been abroad for two months, round the Caribbean," he told them.

"I think that's what we need. A good holiday."

"Go for it, son. We'll be okay here," Tony said. A look passed between father and son and Vicky knew they were up to something, and she smiled to herself.

Later that night people, were dancing and enjoying themselves immensely when David came up to Vicky. "Can I have a word, Vic?" he asked.

She went to the side with him "What's up?"

"Well, you know Maria, is she okay?" he asked her shyly.

"David she is great, and I will let you into a secret, she thinks the world of you," she told him.

"Does she?" he asked, surprised.

"Yes, so if you're going to ask her out to dinner or for a drink, do it, you big oaf," she told him and kissed his cheek, laughing.

Dee had spotted Vicky kissing David, and was seething. Why has she got two hunks tagged onto her, the bitch, she thought. Well, I'm having her husband and she will be the one to lose out. She walked across the room and went over to Eric, putting on all the charm she could. She put her arm through his, and Eric just looked at her.

"What are you doing?" he asked.

"I want you," she said quietly to him.

"Well, I don't want you," he replied.

At that moment Dee didn't realise Mark was behind her, but Eric knew. "What do you say to me and you meeting up and going to a hotel room, and I will show you what real sex is with a real woman, because that wife of yours is probably frigid anyway," she said.

Eric did no more than get his arm away from hers and turn to her. "I love my wife very much and I would never ever cheat on her. You are a disgrace. You're not long married, either," he said to her.

"And she won't be married much longer," Mark piped in.

Dee swung around. "Mark, what are you doing standing there?" she said, shocked.

"Listening to my so-called wife trying to get off with a happily married man," he said.

"I think you had better take her home," Vicky said, coming up behind them and taking Eric's arm. She had heard everything and couldn't believe it. Mark grabbed his wife's arm and literally dragged her out. Not many people had noticed anything.

Eric stood there and wrapped his arms around Vicky. "How long were you stood there?" he asked.

"Long enough," she said, looking up at him and kissing him. The night carried on without another hiccup, and everyone enjoyed themselves. The DJ was playing the last song of the evening, a slow smoochy number. Eric came over to Vicky, who was talking to his mom, and gently pulled her onto the dance floor. He wrapped his arms around her and she him, and they slowly rocked to the music. She put her head on his shoulder and he kissed her hair, smelling everything about her. He loved this woman so much, it hurt sometimes. Vicky pulled back a little, looked up into his eyes and kissed him. They didn't have to say any more; they both knew. They saw everybody off and then David locked up.

Vicky and Eric sat and had a quiet drink after, with David and their mom and dad. "Well, how did you get on with Maria tonight?" Vicky asked David quietly when the others were talking.

He smiled. "I'll tell you both tomorrow," he whispered. Half an hour later, the three of them were walking home. "That's what I call a good night," David said as they walked.

"Yes, it was in the end, wasn't it," Eric said as he held Vicky's hand. David went off to his house, saying goodnight, and they carried on into their driveway and into the house. Once they were in, Vicky kicked off her shoes in the hallway. "Do you want a last drink, sweetheart, before we go up?" Eric asked as he walked into the living room.

"Yes, why not, thanks," she said, following him in. They sat and talked about the night and what happened, but didn't dwell on it because they had both enjoyed it. They finished off their drinks and went upstairs.

Once in the bedroom, Eric went over to Vicky and started kissing her bare shoulders. "I have wanted to do that all night, seeing you in that dress with those bare shoulders and me knowing what's underneath the rest has driven me mad tonight," he said as he started unzipping her dress and kissing her.

"I did notice your eyes following me round the room a few times tonight," she said as she started to unbutton his shirt.

"I couldn't help it," he said as he bent and kissed her neck. They kissed passionately and Vicky undid his trousers and slipped her hand inside, arousing him even more. "Jesus, Vic, you drive me to distraction," he gasped. He let her dress slip down her body to the floor, and then lifted her lovingly onto the bed. By this time Vicky had finished undressing him, and they were both naked on the bed exploring each others' bodies. Vicky sat upon him and he groaned with pleasure while caressing her breasts. She slid off him and kissed him all over; he in turn pressed her to the bed and found the spots on her body that he knew drove her mad when he touched them. He was upon her and entered her once again with passion. They were in rhythm with each other and reached satisfaction together, gripping each others' bodies, never wanting it to end. They fell to sleep spooned together, only wanting and needing each other.

The following day, Sunday, David called round just after dinner. They had arranged staff for today so they could all have the day off. "Afternoon," he said as he breezed in the back door with Tom.

"Blimey, somebody's happy today by the sounds of it," Eric said, looking up from his paper.

David went over and kissed Vicky. "I asked Maria out and she said yes, so we're going for a meal later," he said.

"That's great," Vicky said as she hugged Tom.

"And I suppose you want us to have me laddie here," Eric laughed.

"Well it was in my mind, as I don't think he would like Indian food," David smiled.

"Will you take me to the park later, please, Viddy?" Tom asked. He was five next month but still called Vicky Viddy, as it had just stuck.

"Ooh, I should think we could manage that," Eric said, smiling up at Vicky.

"And afterwards we will take you to the ice cream shop if you're good," Vicky said as she lifted him up.

"Mm, can I have a strawberry one, Dad?" he asked, looking at David.

"Don't ask me, son, Viddy's taking you," he laughed.

"Course you can" she said, giving him a hug and a kiss before she put him down.

***

The next few weeks passed by. Tom had his fifth birthday, and David and Maria sort of fizzled out. They just weren't a good match. But they remained friends. Summer was coming to an end; it was late September when, one Saturday afternoon, Eric answered the door to a familiar face. "Hello Eric," he said.

"Mark! I didn't expect to see you again, come in," he said.

They went into the living room, where Vicky was curled up on the settee. "Sorry if I'm disturbing you," he said.

"No, don't be silly, come and sit down," Vicky said as she uncurled herself.

She looked at Eric and he winked at her. "I'll go and put some coffee on," he said, and went through to the kitchen.

"I had to come and see you both," Mark said when Eric came back in. "Just to apologise if nothing else," he said.

"Why are you apologising?" Eric said.

"Because I'm sorry for what happened at your party."

"But you didn't do anything, Mark," Vicky said as she got up to go and pour the coffee.

"I know, but I was so embarrassed by it all," he said, lowering his head.

"Well, it's all water under the bridge now, so let's forget it," Eric said. Mark went on to tell them that he was now getting divorced but would be staying in the village. Dee had gone back to her parents but she had to talk them into it, because she had let them down and shamed herself. "She told me that she befriended Vicky to get to Eric; she felt sorry for him because of how he looks, thinking that you wouldn't have a very good relationship because of that. But she come unstuck, because she didn't realise just how close you two are," he said, drinking his coffee.

"Well, least you found out early on and not six or seven years down the line, or after you had kids," Eric said to him.

"True," he said. "Anyway, I will leave you in peace, but I wanted to come and let you know that it's only me moved back into the cottage. Will you be in the pub tonight?" he asked.

"Yes, we're both working tonight, Mom and Dad have a weekend off," Eric said.

"I'll see you tonight then," he said as he got up. They both got up with him and walked him to the front door. They said goodbye and closed the door.

"Well, who would have believed it," Eric said as he looked down at Vicky.

"I know, but have you seen the time now? We've got an hour before work," she said as she went to go back in the living room.

"Ooh, grouchy," Eric said as he pulled her to him, kissing her. She just melted in his arms, as usual. How much she loved this man she could never express. He pulled himself away and looked at her smiling. "Better now. I'm going for a shower," he said as he kissed her nose and ran up the stairs. She did no more than follow him up. She wanted him. He had done it again: got rid of her grumps before they had had time to settle. He was so good-humoured. She stripped off in the bedroom and went into the en suite, where Eric was in the shower. She went up behind him, put her arms around his waist and kissed his back. He twisted round and lifted her up to him, kissing her lips tenderly. She wrapped her legs round him and they just kissed. "I want you on the bed," he whispered to her.

She unwrapped herself from round him and they both got out the shower and dried each other off, kissing as they made their way into the bedroom. They fell onto the bed, still damp, and raked each others bodies with their hands, exploring. Eric by now was about to explode with passion; Vicky was the same and they both knew it. He lowered himself onto her; she was gripping his body, pulling him to her, and it excited him even more. "Jesus ,Vicky," he panted. Her breath was hot and fast on his shoulder. The moment came and they both collapsed into each other, relishing every minute. They lay there, getting their breath back.

"I love you, Eric," she whispered into his chest as they lay huddled together.

His arms tightened round her. "I know" was all he needed to say as he kissed her.

They were late getting to the pub for work, but the staff had opened up. They went in like a couple of teenagers, laughing and playing each other up. You wouldn't have thought that they had been married eight years. But the staff they had were good, and they were used to them and got on well. The night went well. Mark came in and they chatted for a while. He was telling Eric that he was looking for a new job, because Dee was still at his old place and it made sense for him to leave.

"Have you ever done building work?" Eric asked.

"I was a labourer when I left school," he said.

"Well, apart from this pub, which you know is a family venture, I also have a building firm down the road, if you're interested," Eric told him.

"Hey, that would be great," he said.

"Come and see me down the yard Monday morning and we'll see what's happening there," Eric said as he went to serve someone.

Vicky was deep in conversation with a man at the other end of the bar. Eric vaguely knew his face, and was curious to who he was. "You okay here, sweetheart?" he asked Vicky as he went down to her.

She turned to him, laughing. "Yes, I'm fine, thanks," she said as she kissed his cheek. "Eric, I would like you to meet Jake. He is an old friend of your father's," she told him.

"Well, nice to meet you Jake, I wondered who you were talking to for so long," he said, looking at Vicky.

"I didn't recognise him. I haven't seen him for fifteen years, just before 'he' died," she told him. "He's come up to see his sister; he's moving up here," she said.

"That's great. Hope to see you in here again, Jake," Eric said as he went to serve again.

"I'm going to have to go, hope to see you soon," she said to him, and went to serve someone else.

"I vaguely remember you mentioning him a few times. We saw him a few times, too, when he used to visit," Eric said to Vicky when they had a break.

"Yes, he was daddy dearest's work mate when he first started work, so he knew him nearly as long as your dad. He had a son, Karl, he was really nice, I used to go to school with him before he stopped me going. He was lovely. I always used to think I would marry him one day. But I was only ten," she said, thinking back.

"What happened to him, then?" Eric asked, detecting the sadness in her voice.

"He was killed. He got knocked down by a joy rider. It was so sad, he was Jake's only son and he was only eleven," she told him.

"I'm sorry," Eric said.

"Yes, it was a really sad affair, it broke his mom's heart. She died two years later, and as far as I know Jake never remarried," she told him.

"Well, why don't you invite him over for lunch or something? Then you can have a proper talk with him. He seems like a really nice bloke," Eric said, getting up. He kissed her cheek and went back behind the bar. Vicky looked over to see Jake just getting up to leave; he waved over to her.

She beckoned him over. "Would you like to come to lunch at our house tomorrow?" she asked.

"No, better not whilst I'm at my sister's," he said.

"Oh, well bring her with you if you like," Vicky said.

He seemed really cagey. "No, that wouldn't do. But I will still come and see you, you were the last person I expected to bump into here," he said. And with that he left, telling her he would see her tomorrow afternoon. Vicky was puzzled. They finished off their shift at the pub and locked up. They poured a drink and went and sat with Dolly and Tony in the bar. There were just the four of them and Vicky was itching to know if Tony remembered Jake, because she hadn't had time to ask him yet.

"Do you remember him, Tony?" Vicky asked at last, being able to talk to him about it.

"Yes, actually I do. Your dad was really pally with him in the early years, and if I remember, he had two sisters. Joan and Alice, I think they were called," he answered.

"Well, one of his sisters lives just outside the village somewhere, he has come to see her., she said.

"I didn't really know him all that well because I didn't work with your dad and him, but him and your dad were mates, then if I remember right, he moved just after you were born," he said, thinking.

"Yes, Dad used to see him about three times a year, I think, but I was only little so I don't remember that much," Vicky said, picking up her drink.

"Did you ask him to lunch?" Eric asked, looking at her.

"Yes, but he was really strange. He said he better not because of his sister, and when I said bring her with him he said that it wouldn't do. Strange, really, I thought," she said.

"Oh, well, maybe she's a funny bugger and he doesn't like taking her anywhere," Tony said, laughing.

All this time Dolly had sat listening. "I remember a Joan at school. What's his surname, this Jake?" she asked.

"Carter," Vicky said, looking at her.

"Yes, that's it. Joan Carter. She went to my school. Jake is about six years older than her, if I remember right, and Alice was younger. So if I'm sixty-five she would be too, and Jake would be seventy-one now. So it could be her that's here; you never know," she said.

"What happened to her, then?" Eric asked.

"She got married when she was about twenty and moved, but I don't know where to. I know she had two children, Peter and Cathy, I think it was," Dolly said thoughtfully.

"Oh well. Come on sweetheart let's get home, it's past midnight and I'm done in," Eric said, getting up and winking at Vicky. They walked home and talked about it some more.

"I might ask him about his sister tomorrow," Vicky said as Eric opened the front door.

When they got inside Eric did his usual thing. He pinned her up the door and kissed her. "Why you have this effect on me, I will never know," he whispered to her as he kissed her.

"I'm glad I do because I like the things you do to me," she whispered back as she responded to his kisses. They worked their way upstairs, undressing each other bit by bit. Once in the bedroom, they were immediately on the bed. They couldn't keep their hands off each other. Eric was kissing her body all over. Vicky was groaning with pleasure. She rolled over and started kissing him, working her way down his body. She loved this man's body, so firm and toned. It turned her on just looking at him.

He pulled her to him and they made love on and off for over an hour, on top of the bed. They fell to sleep entwined in each other as usual, each of them knowing the other was there. The following morning Vicky woke first, and got up and went downstairs. She picked the clothes up off the stairs on her way down, smiling as she remembered the night before just like Eric did. She made some tea and toast, and went back upstairs to bed. Eric was still asleep. He looked so peaceful lying there on his stomach, his muscular body lying across the bed. She knelt on the bed and kissed his back all the way up his spine.

He slowly turned and saw her there, naked apart from his shirt that was undone at the front. She looked gorgeous. He pulled her over to him and gently and lovingly caressed her body, making her crazy for him. They had passionate sex, so in love with each other they just blended together. Later on that day, they were cuddled up on the settee when the doorbell rang.

"I bet that's Jake," Eric said as he got up. A few minutes later Eric came back in with Jake.

"I'm glad you came. Would you like some coffee?" Vicky said to him.

"Yes, that would be nice, thank you," he answered as he sat down. Eric disappeared into the kitchen to put the coffee on. "How are you anyway, Vicky?" he asked.

"I'm good, thank you; it's so nice to see you again after all this time."

Just then Eric came in with the coffee. "I just about remember you, Jake, from when you used to visit, but I wasn't very old so can't remember much, I'm afraid, just that you used to visit your sister and her kids or something like that," he said.

"Yes, that's right," he said, picking up his coffee.

"Cathy and Peter, wasn't it. Mom said she vaguely remembered them. She went to school with Joan, apparently."

"Yes, she did. I remember your mom."

"Where do they live now, then? Are they around here too?" Vicky asked.

"No, Peter's married with two kids and lives in Ireland. And Cathy went to live in Wales and stayed there after the adoption, to li... sorry, shouldn't have said that." And he clammed up.

"What, was Cathy adopted? Is that what you're saying?" Vicky asked.

"No, she and Peter are Jean's kids" he told them.

"So Cathy had a baby adopted and then went to Wales?" Eric asked.

"Oh God, she is going to kill me," Jake said, looking into his cup.

"Sorry Jake, it's not really any of our business," Eric apologised.

"No, it's fine really, its been in my head for years, I don't think she should have done it, I didn't agree with it one bit," he said, still looking into his cup.

"What you didn't agree with the adoption?" Vicky asked.

"No, I said to Jean that she could have brought the child up as her own, but she wanted to punish Cathy for getting pregnant. She brought shame on her mom, that's all Jean was bothered about. All she has ever been bothered about. And because she was only fourteen Cathy had no say in it. Cathy hasn't had anything to do with her mom since. It's been twenty-nine years since they spoke or saw each other," he said sadly.

"So somewhere out there she has a grandchild she cares nothing about?" Vicky asked.

"Yes that's the be all and end all of it," he said.

"Do you know where the baby went, or if it was a boy or a girl?" Eric asked.

"It was a bonny little girl with a mass of dark hair. I saw her when she was born. I was the only one to go and see Cathy," he said sadly.

"That's terrible," Vicky said. "Has Cathy ever tried to find her?" she asked.

"No, she's wanted to loads of times, but thinks she would be rejected and couldn't stand that. She never had any more kids. But I think they have both got a right to know, but it's not my place to say," he told them.

"So you know where the baby went to?" Eric asked.

"Yes, I do," he answered as he got up to go. "I must be off now. Jean will wonder where I am and I haven't told her where I am," he said. Vicky and Eric just looked at each other and frowned. They saw him out and went down the pub to see Dolly and Tony, not giving much thought to what Jake had said, really.

CHAPTER SEVEN

It was now coming up to Christmas, one of the busiest times of the year. Everyone was flat out, sorting orders and taking bookings for meals. "Shall we have everybody over to the house for Christmas dinner this year?" Vicky said to Eric as he sorted behind the bar. He stopped and looked round at her, seeing the sparkle in her eyes. He walked round the other side of the bar and kissed her. "What was that for?" she smiled up at him.

"Just for being you," he said as he kissed her again.

She looked up at him. "Well, after you have finished driving me crazy, will you answer my question, please?"

He looked down at her. "Driving you crazy, am I?" he said teasingly.

"You know you do when you do things like that, so stop teasing and answer me," she said, kissing his cheek.

"Okay, okay. Yes, let's have everyone over, as long as I get my Christmas morning with my wife and can have her to myself for a couple of hours," he said, kissing her again and smiling at her.

"Tease," she said, smiling, and walked off into the kitchen, looking back and blowing him a kiss. He smiled to himself. God he loved that woman.

Christmas Eve was here and the pub was packed. They had a disco in the function room and a Christmas quiz in the bar. They were all working behind the bar tonight, Mom, Dad, Eric, Vicky and David, plus three bar staff. They were run off their feet. Sarah was in the lounge with Tom, who was now five and a half.; he had been told he could stay up until 9 pm if he was good.

Vicky loved Christmas. She could get to spend time with Tom and spoil him. She loved him to bits, and they were really close. The disco was packed, and Vicky and David were behind the bar serving. "I will be glad to have a break," David shouted above the music.

"So will I," Vicky replied. Nine o'clock came and Vicky helped Sarah upstairs with Tom.

"It's like a madhouse down there tonight," Vicky said to Sarah.

"Viddy, will you read me a story please?" Tom asked.

"I can't tonight, but Sarah will. I'll read you one tomorrow night, okay?" and she kissed him goodnight as she put him into bed.

Tom was sharing a room with his dad tonight and knew Santa was coming, so he was on his best behaviour. "Okay, you promise?" he asked.

"Have I ever broken a promise to you yet?" Vicky said softly as she tucked him in and kissed him.

He smiled up at her with sleepy eyes. "I'll have to go down now, will you be down in a bit?" Vicky asked Sarah, who was just sorting out Tom's clothes.

"Yes, I'll just make sure he's settled and I will be down. I'll come and check him every twenty minutes," she said as she tucked Tom into his bed again.

Back downstairs, Vicky went and found Eric. "Hi sweetheart, you okay?" he asked as he was serving.

"Yes, I'm fine. Are you having a break soon?" she asked him as she helped him serve some people.

"Yes, just waiting for David and Dad to come back. You coming with me?" he said, winking at her. She gave him a cheeky smile and carried on serving. Ten minutes later Tony and David came back and they went for their break together. "What a night," Eric said when they were stood out the back with a drink each.

"Yes, it's going well," she said as she reached up and kissed him.

"Missed you though," he said to her as he responded to her kiss. They just stood in the darkness holding each other, enjoying the fresh air.

Christmas and New Year were over. It was now 1995. They had had a fabulous Christmas. The pub had done really well, and all the locals congratulated them for a wonderful time. January came to an end and things got back to normal. Vicky had started to spend a bit of time at her office. Stuart, her manager, was still there and welcomed her back. Eric was spending more time at his yard now, too. They had stepped back a bit from their businesses to get the pub in order, and had never really got back, but they both decided to try and get back to normal now, as the pub was doing okay and David was there now most of the time. Lunch times went back to the old ways too, which Eric said was the best bit of going back to the yard. They would meet up at the house but nearly always ended up having no lunch, because they were too interested in undressing each other.

June came round, and so did their tenth anniversary. Eric decided to take Vicky away, but hadn't told her what he had planned. David knew and did all the arrangements for Eric so as not to give the game away. Wednesday night when they were on the settee watching the TV, Eric told Vicky they were going away Saturday.

"Oh, Eric, that's wonderful. But that only gives me two days to sort myself out," she said in panic.

"Don't worry, you've got a whole two days because you're not at work and Sarah is going to help you," he said as he kissed her.

"You have been busy, haven't you?" she said cheekily as she climbed on top of him on the settee and sat on him.

"Yes, well, ten years with the woman I idolise is worth celebrating in style," he said as he put his hands round her waist and looked up at her.

"Are you going to tell me where we're going?" she asked as she leaned forward and kissed him.

"No, so don't keep asking. It's a surprise. But you will need your costume and evening dresses. Oh, and some sexy underwear will definitely be a bonus," he said, smiling up at her.

"A bonus for who. You?" she laughed. She slid her legs down his and was laying on top of him, looking down at him. "Eric Armstrong, I must be the luckiest woman alive. Thank you. I love you," she said as she put her head on his chest and he wrapped his arms round her.

They lay there for a bit when suddenly Eric rolled off the settee, pulling her down with him. "Undress me, Vic, I want you," he said as he grappled with her buttons. She responded like clockwork because she knew when he called her Vic that his body was on a high. In no time, they were in rhythm and melting against each other. The sex was hot and fiery, just like she expected it would be. They lay there in each others' arms, breathless.

***

Saturday came and they were awake early. Eric went down to make some tea and Vicky got in the shower. When he came back up he did his usual thing and got in the shower with her, and went up behind her. "These next two weeks I am going to love you every day like never before," he said as he kissed her shoulders and neck.

She turned to him. "You couldn't love me any better; you spoil me already and I love you for it," she said as she reached up and kissed him.

"My darling Vicky. I have loved you probably for most of my life. Ten of those years have been the best of my life, for being married to you. Some time was wasted because we were too scared to say anything to each other, and not seeing you. But now I couldn't love you more. You mean the world to me and I can't get enough of you," he said, lowering his head and kissing her lips.

"You have always said the most wonderful things to me. You are my world too. Every part of me aches for you everyday. I love you so much," she said, succumbing to his touch. They made love there in the shower with a passion that burnt. They waved goodbye to everybody at 9 am, when David came to run them to their destination. Eric still wouldn't tell her where they were going.

"I suppose you know, don't you," Vicky said to David, laughing.

"Of course," he replied as he pulled off the pub car park.

They arrived in Southampton an hour and a half later. "Well, Mrs Armstrong. This is your first destination," Eric told her, pointing up at a cruise liner after David had dropped them off and said goodbye.

"A cruise. Oh, Eric, thank you," she said with tears in her eyes, kissing him and throwing her arms round him.

"You deserve the best, so you are having it and I told you, I am going to love you like never before," he said, wiping away her tears and kissing her. He picked up their suitcases and found a porter. They booked onto the ship and walked up the gangway. It was incredible. They were shown to their cabin. Eric had booked them in the honeymoon suite. It was exquisite. They unpacked their things and went back upon deck, ready for the off. They stood by the rails and Vicky was leaning back against Eric, and he had his arms around her.

She rested her head against his strong arms. "I love you," she told him quietly.

He bent his head down to her and kissed her cheek. "I know," was all he needed to say. The first night they walked round hand in hand, and got to know the ship. There was everything you could think of on here. They were going to have the time of their lives. They went into one of the bars for a drink, then went and got changed for dinner. Their cabin was wonderful, with a view out to sea that took your breath away. "Well, how is it fairing so far," Eric asked as he undressed her in their cabin.

"Oh, Eric, it's wonderful. Just like you," she said, kissing him longingly. Within minutes they were on the bed, christening it with their love. An hour later they were walking down to dinner. The restaurant was enormous. They met an older couple, Grant and Hilary, and got talking to them; they were really nice. They dined with them and drank with them afterwards. He was forty-nine and a company director, and she was forty-seven and a housewife. They had three grown-up children, two sons and a daughter, and two grandchildren, and had been married for twenty-six years. Eric and Vicky filled in the gaps about themselves and Grant couldn't believe they had been married for ten years, as they were so much in love.

"What's your secret?" Hilary asked Vicky when the men went up the bar.

"Nothing really. We just love each other," she replied simply.

"Can I ask you a question?" Hilary said.

"Yes, of course. Whether I answer depends on what you ask," Vicky said, smiling.

Hilary laughed. "Of course. But what happened to Eric's face?" she asked curiously.

Vicky looked over to Eric, who was up the bar, and Hilary saw the look of love and admiration in her eyes. "You don't have to tell me, I can see it's painful for you. I'm sorry," she said softly.

"No, it's fine, really," Vicky said, warming to this kind woman. She told her about the accident and the baby, the miscarriage before and about her accident.

"Oh, Vicky, that's awful for you. I'm so sorry," she said as she leaned over and rubbed her hand.

"It's a long time ago now, but it still hurts sometimes and Eric is wonderful, he really is," Vicky said as the men walked back over with their drinks.

"We should have got the waiter, it would have been quicker," Grant said, laughing, as they sat down.

Eric put his arm around Vicky's shoulder and hugged her. Hilary couldn't believe just how much they had been through, and still loved each other like they did. Most couples would have cracked and split up a long time ago. "You okay, sweetheart?" he asked as he passed her her drink.

"Mm, wonderful," she said as she sipped it. They all made arrangements to meet tomorrow morning in the restaurant again, and then they were going to spend the day together when they went ashore in Egypt. The four of them got on really well. A few hours and a few drinks later, they said goodnight and found their way back to their cabins. Once back in theirs, Vicky kicked off her shoes and threw herself on the bed. Eric stood there laughing, seeing how happy she was. They had both had a bit to drink but weren't drunk, just merry.

"Why don't you get yourself on here with me, Mr Armstrong," Vicky said, reaching over to grab his hand and trying to pull him down.

"Don't worry, I'm coming," he said, kneeling on the bed and leaning over her. "Are you happy and enjoying yourself sweetheart?" he asked as he bent to kiss her.

"I couldn't ask to be happier," she said, wrapping her arms round his neck and pulling him down. He collapsed on top of her and they both burst out laughing, rolling over on the bed. Eric seductively started to undress her and she looked up at him, smiling, letting his hands roam over her body.

"I told you I was going to love you like never before and I meant every word," he whispered to her as he bit gently at her neck. Vicky groaned with pleasure and she started to undress him. By now she was completely naked and Eric was working his way down her body, kissing every part of it. He kissed the parts that he, and only he, knew drove her crazy, and she arched her back, pulling at him. He worked his way back up to her mouth and kissed her longingly. "I love you so much," he said softly.

By now, Vicky was desperate for him. She gripped him to her and could feel the hardness of his body. Eric was trying to play the waiting game but was finding it extremely difficult, as he was also desperate for her. Her hands felt like velvet caressing his body, and every inch of him tingled. He turned her over so as she was on her stomach, and took her from behind. She pushed herself upon to her knees and he onto his; she then pushed back onto him and they both groaned with sheer pleasure as the force of their need erupted, and they exploded together as they made love with a longing so strong their hearts ached for each other like never before. They collapsed exhausted into a heap on the bed and silently fell to sleep, encased in each other.

The following morning they showered together and dressed, ready to go for breakfast. "I do like Grant and Hilary, they are so easy to get on with and she is so warm and genuine," Vicky said as they strolled down towards the restaurant arm in arm.

"Yes, he's the same. A really genuine bloke," Eric said.

They stopped by the railings. The sea air was wonderful and the sun was baking down on them already. They stood and held each other for a few moments, kissed and carried on, Eric with his arm round her shoulders. "I love you, Eric," she said as they walked.

He squeezed her shoulders with his arm and lowered his head "I know," he whispered.

Hilary and Grant were already there. They had ordered some tea and coffee and were just buttering some toast. "Good morning," they said as they sat down.

"Morning, sleep well?" Grant asked as he bit on his toast.

"Like a log," Eric replied as he poured some tea.

"What about you, Vicky?" Hilary asked.

"Yes like a log too. I couldn't believe it when I woke up at seven-thirty," she said, smiling across the table at her. They all ordered breakfast and before they knew it, the ship was docked in Cairo. They had the most wonderful day, exploring the markets and looking at the sights. They had got to know each other better, too, and got on really well. They got back on the ship and parted to go to their cabins, arranging to meet up later on before dinner, for a drink.

The rest of the two weeks were the same. They enjoyed themselves immensely. Eric had kept his word, too. He had loved Vicky everyday like never before. She hadn't thought it possible, but found herself loving him even more. They had made love or had hot fiery sex two or three times a day every day, and every day was different, just like Eric had said it would be. The holiday was at an end now, and they were on their way back to Southampton. They had exchanged phone numbers and addresses with Grant and Hilary, and had arranged for them to come and stay at the house in a week's time. They actually got off the ship about 3 pm, and eventually got their luggage. They said goodbye to Grant and Hilary and went and found David, who had come to pick them up.

"Welcome home," he said, wrapping his arms round Vicky and giving Eric a brotherly hug.

"Nice to be home," Eric said, looking down at a bronzed Vicky and smiling. She looked lovely. They told David all about it on the journey home, asking about everyone in between. They got back home just before teatime. They did their rounds of hugs and kisses, and gave everyone their presents. With all the formalities out the way they went home, telling everyone they would see them later for a drink. They got in the house and closed the door behind them.

"Thank you for a wonderful holiday," Vicky said as she reached up and kissed Eric, pulling him to her.

He wrapped his arms around her and responded to her kiss. "Thank you too," he whispered. They were unpacked and sorted within a couple of hours. They were getting ready to go down the pub when the phone rang.

"Hello, is that Eric?"

"Yes. Is that you, Grant?"

"Yes. Just to let you know we won't be able to do a week's time with you. I forgot we had a prior dinner engagement. Would two weeks suit you?" he asked.

"Yes, that's fine. No problem. Thanks for letting us know. Glad to be home, are you?" Eric asked.

"Oh yes, wonderful," he replied sarcastically. They both laughed and said goodbye. Eric relayed it to Vicky.

"Oh, that's a shame, but never mind," she said, coming over to him. He looked at her and could see the look in her eyes.

"Are you about to misbehave and take me for granted?" he asked as he put his arms round her and kissed her.

"What gives you that idea?" she said, smiling up at him and taking his hand.

"The fact that you are in just your sexy underwear and leading me towards the bed, tempting me," he said, reaching out for her.

"It's your own fault. You have treated me too well on holiday. Now I have got to pay you back," she said as she pulled him onto the bed and seriously seduced him. Later that evening, they walked down to the Thistle. It was good to be back and good to see the family again. They sat with David, who wasn't working tonight, and told him about Grant and Hilary.

"They sound like a nice couple," he said.

"Anything been happening here" Eric asked.

"No, not really. Oh, yes: Jake came in looking for you, Vicky. I told him you were back today, so he will probably see you tomorrow or Monday," David told them as he got up to get some more drinks.

Last orders were called and Eric and Vicky left to go home, saying goodnight to everyone. "I feel drained," Vicky said as they walked home.

"Have I wore you out?" Eric said, laughing as he put his arm round her. She playfully punched him and ran off in front of him. He chased her to the front door, where they ended up kissing breathlessly.

"I've still got some energy left so beware, Mr Armstrong," she said as he opened the door.

"I can't wait," he smiled as the door shut behind them.

***

Two weeks later, Grant and Hilary arrived for the weekend. "It's so lovely to see you again," Hilary said as she hugged Vicky. Eric and Grant hit it off again and were deep in conversation about a variety of subjects. It was the beginning of a wonderful friendship that would last for many years. The months flew past and before they knew it, it was nearly Christmas again. Eric and Vicky had grown even closer since their holiday, and they were getting on great with Hilary and Grant. They stayed at each others' houses for the weekend, taking it in turns once a month. Christmas they were coming to them, because of the pub.

***

All the preparations were in order and David decided to take a few days holiday with Tom before the Christmas celebrations started. Hilary and Grant invited him up to theirs, as they had fallen in love with Tom. They got on well and David liked them both. He went with no hesitation. They welcomed David and Tom with open arms when they got there. They planned their days. Tom was being whisked off to go Christmas shopping with Hilary. He was now five and a half, and as wise as a forty-year-old. David was going to have a well-earned rest and lounge about with Grant. He loved it. The day before David was due to go home, Hilary and Grant's daughter Lynn came to see them. She had broken up from work for Christmas, and came to see them before she went to her brothers. Grant introduced them to each other and she immediately took to Tom, like her mother had.

"He's lovely," she said to David shyly.

David noticed she had the greenest eyes he had ever seen. "Thank you," he replied.

"Mom tells me that you are bringing him up on your own," she said, looking at him.

"Yes, well, not entirely, my brother Eric and his wife Vicky play a big part in his life, always have. Vicky is like the mom he never had. She's great, they're inseparable. And having his nan and granddad round him so much has helped as well," he told her.

"Mom has told me about Eric and Vicky, she loves Vicky like another daughter. Says they have been through so much, yet they are inseparable too."

"Yes they are. They're a great couple. They have a special bond between them that nothing can get through, and I love them both," he said, thinking.

"Well, one day I might meet them myself when they are here," she said, looking at him again. She found him fascinating. His build made him look sexy, and he was so polite and considerate. Just wonderful, really, she thought.

That night in bed, Lynn found herself thinking about David. He was lovely, he really was. She had become smitten with him. She had to think of an excuse to be able to see him again. The following morning they were all at breakfast. David was looking forward to seeing Lynn again, but he was looking forward to going home now as well. "Are you busy all over Christmas?" he asked Lynn quietly when they were alone in the kitchen.

"No, not really, I can please myself what I do."

"Would you consider driving up to Little Haven for the New Year? You could stay with Mom and Dad if you didn't want to stay at mine."

She gave it some thought, but not for too long. "I would love that. Thank you," she answered.

Later on, he and Tom were on their way home. "I like Lynn," Tom suddenly piped up.

"Good. Glad you do. She's coming up for the New Year so you can see her again," David said as he too thought about her. They arrived home the day before Christmas Eve. Tom had to go straight to see Vicky. She and Eric were at the pub with Mom and Dad.

"Hello trouble," Vicky said as Tom ran to her and threw his arms round her. He then did the same to his nan. David told them all about Lynn and her coming up to join her mom and dad New Year's Eve. When they got home, Eric and Vicky were talking about it. "I do hope David gets to have a bit of happiness," Vicky said as they got in.

"So do I. I wish he could be as happy as we are," Eric said as they went into the kitchen.

"Me too. But if they do get on and it goes on, I just hope that she gets on with Tom," Vicky said.

"And me. Because I won't see him upset," Eric said thoughtfully. He went up behind her and put his arms round her as she started to prepare their dinner. He stood holding her. "Grant and Hilary have told us a lot about her, and she sounds really nice. But we will see for ourselves next week," he said as he kissed her neck and went to get the wine for dinner. They wasn't working tonight; they were having a night off and stopping in because they were working tomorrow night, Christmas Eve.

After their dinner they curled up together on the sofa and watched the TV. Eric's hands began to wander. Vicky laughed and slapped his wrist and told him to behave, but to no avail. "How do you expect me to behave when I've lay here for the last hour with your warm soft body next to me?" he said as he kissed the top of her head.

Vicky twisted round to face him. "Eric Armstrong, will you ever be able to control yourself?" she said, looking into his eyes and smiling.

"I hope not," he said seductively. He hugged her to him and they started slowly undressing each other, kissing and teasing as they went, undoing buttons and belts, hands everywhere.

136

They made love on the sofa, then lay contented in each other's arms and finished off the wine. This sort of night was what they both loved best.

Christmas Eve afternoon, Grant and Hilary arrived. They were staying with Vicky and Eric as usual. They were going to sit up the end of the bar whilst Eric and Vicky worked tonight; they had done it many times and were used to it, and didn't mind at all. In fact, they enjoyed watching all the banter that went on.

"I can't believe Lynn's coming for the New Year to see David," Hilary said to Vicky when they were in the kitchen making coffee.

"Yes, he told us," Vicky replied.

"Well I know it's early days yet, but I hope they hit it off, because he is lovely and so is Tom. Lynn thinks the world of Tom, so you've got no worries there," Hilary told her.

Vicky was thoughtful. She was so used to having Tom virtually to herself, she found herself scared of losing him. But she then told herself off for being stupid.

Christmas came and went. Christmas dinner was a success, with everybody round the table enjoying themselves and having their fill. It was now New Year's Eve and David found himself on tenterhooks waiting to see Lynn. He called in to see Vicky; she always managed to calm him down about things. He greeted everybody as he walked in, then went over to Vicky.

"Can I have a word," he asked her quietly. Eric saw this and knew what was wrong with his brother. He winked over at Vicky, and then side-tracked Hilary and Grant so they wouldn't notice just how nervous David was about seeing their daughter. Vicky and David disappeared into the living room.

"Vicky, I'm so nervous about seeing her. What if she's gone off me, or if she doesn't like what she sees a second time?" he said.

"David, stop babbling and don't talk so wet. If she does either of those things, and I don't think she will, then she needs her head testing. You are a wonderful man just like your brother, that's why I love you so much. So stop worrying," she said, and gave him a big hug.

He looked down at her. "I wish I could meet someone who comes even halfway as good as you," he said.

"Well, Lynn doesn't sound that bad and Tom likes her, so that's a bonus already," she answered as they made their way back into the kitchen.

"Thanks, Vicky. You always manage to calm me down somehow," he said. Eric looked at them as they came back in, and he could see his brother was a lot calmer now that his precious wife had worked her magic.

At one-thirty that afternoon, Lynn pulled onto the drive. Hilary and Grant went straight out to her. Vicky and Eric stood on the step and welcomed her in. "It's so nice to meet you at last. I've heard so much about you both from Mom and Dad. And David was praising you both up when I saw him, too," Lynn said as they went into the living room.

"It's nice to meet you at last, too. And I hope that you enjoy yourself while you're here," Vicky said as she went back into the kitchen to make some coffee.

"You are most definitely Eric," Lynn said to him, smiling.

"Yes, that's me." he said, smiling back.

"There's no mistaking you're David's brother, is there?" she laughed.

"No, like two peas in a pod," Vicky said as she walked back in with the coffee. They sat and talked for a while, getting to know each other, and then Grant and Hilary said they were going to see Dolly and Tony. Just as they were going, David turned up.

"Where's Tom?" Lynn asked.

"I left him with Sarah for a bit, so we can have a bit of peace," he laughed. The four of them chatted and got on really well. Lynn was just as warm and friendly as her mom, Vicky thought.

New Year's Eve night was upon them, and they were getting ready to go out. Vicky and Eric weren't working that night;

neither was David. "Well. What do you think of her?" Eric asked Vicky as they got ready.

"She seems really nice. But she had better not hurt David. He's been through enough," she said sadly.

"Hey, come on, you," Eric said as he wrapped his arms round her.

"I know. I'm sorry. It's just that I sometimes feel so sorry for him. He hasn't been very lucky in love, has he? And he deserves it," she said, looking up at him.

He bent his head down and kissed her. "I think I had all the luck when you told me that you loved me. I was elated when that happened, and I will never forget the day," he said.

"No, me neither. You told me you loved me and my heart jumped for joy," she said, remembering.

"Yes, I remember that feeling too," he smiled.

"I could have sang from the hill tops when you did, though."

"No regrets, then?" he asked, holding her.

"How could I ever have any regrets about marrying you? You are my gentle giant and I love you to bits," she said, hugging him.

"Yes, well, we had better get ready. I only wish I could ravish you here and now. I want to, believe me, but with Hilary and Grant on the move across the landing I'll wait till later; then I can really take advantage of you, Mrs Armstrong," he said, kissing her again.

"Don't," she said, looking up at him. "I'm going to be thinking of that all night now, and it's going to drive me crazy and its going to be a long night." She could feel the hardness of him against her, and it was turning her on. "I don't think I can wait until we come home, Eric," she said, undoing his belt and slipping her hand into his trousers.

"Oh God, Vicky. The things you do to me," he groaned, and pulled off her blouse. They were on the bed in seconds, pumping each others' bodies and releasing all the frustration. They lay there breathless against each other. "You are a bad influence on me, Vicky Armstrong." Eric said as he kissed her and got up.

"Mm, but you like it, don't you. You never complain," she said as he pulled her off the bed and she kissed him. He kissed her nose and gave her a cheeky grin.

***

The party went well and they saw in 1996 in style. Lynn was a really good laugh when she was out, and Vicky really liked her. "How are you two getting on?" she asked David.

"Very well. She's great fun and I really like her," he said.

"I can see that. I think she is a bit smitten with you," Vicky told him.

"Really!" He smiled down at her, raising his eyebrows. With the party coming to an end and people starting to leave, they started to clear up a bit.

"Would you like some help?" Lynn asked Vicky.

"Thanks. The more help, the quicker it gets done," she replied.

In the pub kitchen, Eric was throwing the empties into the bottle bin. He turned round to see Vicky watching him. "What's up, sweetheart?" he asked.

"Nothing. I just like looking at you sometimes," she said as she walked over to him and put her arms up round his neck. "Happy New Year. I love you." She gently kissed him.

"Same to you and I love you too, even more than last year," he smiled at her. They stood there for a while holding each other; then Lynn walked in with a tray full of glasses.

"Oh I'm sorry." she said to them just as David came in behind her.

"Don't worry about them two, Lynn. They are always like that," he laughed.

"Take no notice of him," Vicky said as she playfully slapped him. They cleared most of the mess away between them all, and left the rest for the following day. They all had a nightcap, said goodnight to Dolly and Tony, and went to Eric and Vicky's house. Grant and Hilary went to bed after about half an hour.

"Are you stopping here with your mom and dad?" David asked Lynn quietly.

She turned and smiled at him. "Not if you don't want me to," she said, looking up at him.

"No, I don't, really. You could always stay at mine. I've got a spare bed if you want it."

"Spare bed indeed," she whispered to him, smiling. They got up to leave.

"We're off now," David told Eric and Vicky, and they smiled at each other. When all was quiet, Eric took hold of Vicky and carried her up the stairs. They christened 1996 with their love for one another and fell to sleep in each others' arms.

CHAPTER EIGHT

They were now nearing the millennium. Vicky and Eric had been married for fourteen years. David was married to Lynn and had been for two years. They had hit it off so well that within six months they were married. They also had a ten-month-old baby girl called Davina, after her dad. Tom was now nearly eleven, and nearly at senior school. He still thought the world of Vicky and told her everything. He also got on well with Lynn and liked her a lot, but Vicky was his leaning post and always would be, as far as he was concerned. Nobody minded this, as they all knew he had always looked upon her as the mom he never had. He loved his little sister, though, and always made a fuss over her.

The Golden Thistle was still doing well, but they now had a manager in there so they could all take a bit of a back seat. Dolly and Tony had retired. They eventually sold their house and brought a cottage in the village, just up the road from them. It was October and everything was good. "Do you fancy going away for a few days?" Eric asked Vicky one night when they were lying on the settee watching TV, cocooned in one another. Their love for each other had never faltered. Even though they had had their fair share of heartaches, they loved each other as much now as they did when they first got married, if not more.

"Where do you want to go then? Have you anywhere in mind?" she said as she turned round to face him.

He brushed her hair away from her face with his fingers and kissed her. "Anywhere, as long as it's just us two. I want you to myself for a few days or longer, if possible. I'm not complaining because I love everybody to bits, but just lately we never seem to be alone for very long, do we?" he said, looking into her eyes.

"I know. I miss having you to myself, too. There's always someone wanting you for something or other and that's not a complaint either, but sometimes I want you too but someone else has got you," she said as she touched his scarred cheek. They kissed each other with a longing. Eric had just begun to unbutton her blouse and she his trousers when the doorbell rang.

"Oh God, not now," Eric gasped as he pulled away to get up, kissing Vicky as he did and pulling her up too. "What were we saying?" he said as he did up his trousers and put himself straight. Vicky smiled at him and blew him a kiss as he went to answer the door. He came back into the living room followed by David and Lynn. "We thought we would come and see if you want to come for a drink," David said as he looked at Eric.

"No, not tonight, mate. I'm done in. What about you, Vic?" he said, looking at her with longing in his eyes. She was already going to say no anyway because she didn't want to tonight; all she wanted was Eric. But she also knew what it meant when he called her Vic. He was burning for her and she knew it.

"No. I'm good tonight as well, thanks."

"Okay. But we will make a date for Saturday if you want, because Grant and Hilary are having the kids overnight," David said as they moved back into the hall.

"Yes, that will be great," Vicky said. They closed the door behind them and Eric was all over her like a rash. God, how she loved this man. The door was barely shut and he had her pinned against it, pulling at her clothes and kissing her.

"Undress me like you do, Vic," he whispered in her ear. His breath was hot on her neck and his hands were all over her. She pulled off his shirt and kissed his chest, working her way down to his waist, undoing his trousers; he was aroused for her, and she was mad for him. He pulled her back up to him, and she put her arms around his neck and wrapped her legs round his waist as he held her. They had frenzied sex against the front door, gripping each others' bodies, reaching the heights they were so desperate for together. They stayed there for a few minutes getting their breath back; then he gently lowered her and kissed her like there was no tomorrow.

"I love you so much. We need to get away for a few days, so we can spend some time together properly. I want to have time to love you, sweetheart," he said as he picked her up and carried her into the living room.

"I need to love you, I long for your touch most of the time," she said as he wrapped a throw round her naked body and she held him tight. "I will see what I can sort out tomorrow," she said against his chest. They lay back on the settee spooned together, never wanting to let go.

Two days later, on Sunday morning, they left to drive down to the coast for seven days away. Everybody told them to have a good rest and come back recharged. Eric drove off, and at last they were totally on their own. They arrived later that afternoon and, having booked into their hotel and unpacked, they went and had a walk along the beach. This time they didn't want to be bothered by anyone. They just wanted to be alone and spend time with each other. They went back to the hotel in time to get changed for their evening meal at seven.

Up in the room Eric was shaving, but he was watching Vicky in the mirror and he could see her flinching when she moved. He didn't say anything then, but he was going to keep an eye on her. She would tell him if there was a problem. He finished shaving and went and put his arms gently round her. "Are you okay, sweetheart?" he asked.

"I am now I've got you to myself," she said, kissing him. They went downstairs ten minutes later for their meal. But she still hadn't said anything, so Eric thought no more of it. Maybe it was just a twinge. He would watch her, though.

They had had a wonderful four days so far and had explored each other's bodies from top to bottom as if they didn't know them. Thursday morning Eric woke. He looked at Vicky, still asleep on her stomach. He kissed her back all up her spine. She didn't flinch. "Vicky," he whispered in her ear. Still nothing. "Vicky," he said, louder. Still nothing. He leaned over her and could hear her shallow breathing, but he couldn't wake her. He phoned the main desk and asked for an ambulance after numerous attempts to wake her. While he waited for someone to come, he managed to get her into one of his shirts, because she was naked. He sat and held her limp body, and cried.

The ambulance came in ten minutes; they checked her over and took her straight to hospital. They said she seemed to be in a coma but they didn't know why, and they were going to give her a brain scan to see if they could see anything. He sat and waited; then, suddenly, thought he'd better call home. After he had relayed everything to them, David told him he was coming down to him.

"I was there for you before and I'm here for you now; I'll see you in a while," he told him, and was gone. Two hours later David walked into the hospital. "Have you heard any more?" he asked Eric as he reached him. He looked awful.

"No, not yet, they are doing a scan and when they get the results they will let me know." Just then a doctor came out to them.

"Mr Armstrong?" he asked.

"Yes, that's me," Eric said.

"I don't know how to tell you this really, but your wife has a brain tumour," he said.

Eric nearly collapsed. "Oh God no," he cried.

"We are going to do a biopsy and then we will know if we can operate or not," he told them. "Has she ever had a bad bang to the head or anything?"

David and Eric looked at each other. They told the doctor about her car accident years ago, and about her dad beating her to a pulp. "That's when it probably started growing. It is the size of a golf ball on the left-hand side of her brain," he said.

Eric had to sit down. He couldn't take it in. "What will happen to her?" he asked.

"If we can operate, she should eventually make a full recovery. But if we can't, her motivation and speech will get worse and, I'm sorry, but it will eventually kill her," he said softly. "I will keep you informed," he told them as he walked away.

Both of them sat there in shock. Early the following morning, after they had both had a sleepless night in the waiting area, the doctor came out to them. "Mr Armstrong. We are going to be able to operate on your wife but it will be very dangerous for her, as it's a tricky operation. The odds are that she should make a recovery, but we can't say for certain," he told them. "She will be going down to theatre in half an hour. You can go and see her for a few minutes before."

"Thank you," Eric said, still in shock. They both walked in to see her, and all the memories from before came flooding back to Eric. She was covered in tubes and lying motionless. He kissed her lips and willed her to come back to him again.

Four hours later the doctor came to see them. "We think that everything has gone well. But time will tell and it's just a case of waiting now, I'm afraid. We have completely removed the tumour and all is clear now, so we will have to wait and see. You should be able to go and sit with her soon," he told them.

Eric shook his hand. "Thank you, doctor," he said, and with that the doctor went. He fell down on the seat, put his head in his hands and wept. David put his arm round his shoulders and just held him. Within two hours they could go in and see her. They had had to shave part of her head, and it was bandaged up. She lay there and she looked so small and vulnerable, Eric thought. He leaned over her and gently kissed her cheek "Please come back to me. I love you," he whispered to her.

Four days later Vicky was still in a coma. They took her for another scan to make sure all was clear, and nothing was found. They said she should come round in her own time now. David had gone home and come back again. They had both been to the hotel, and Eric had booked out and got their things. As he looked round the room, he remembered the loving they had had there. He closed the door and went down.

He stayed at the hospital at Vicky's bedside; she was in a private room now. It had been a week since she came in. The doctors said she was doing all right, but she still hadn't woken up. Friday morning came and Eric and David were just going to get some air and a coffee when Vicky's eyes opened. She looked round the room and at Eric, but didn't say anything.

David fetched the nurse. She checked Vicky over and spoke softly to her, but Vicky just looked around her. She told them she was going to get the doctor; there was nothing wrong apart form her recognition and that she hadn't spoken. She left the room and Vicky stared at them both. Eric took her hand. "It's okay, sweetheart. The doctor's coming," he said, but she still just stared at him as if she didn't recognise him.

The doctor arrived and Eric and David left the room so he could completely check her over. "What do you think's wrong?" Eric said to David as they were getting yet another coffee.

"Hopefully nothing," he said, looking at his brother. He suddenly noticed that Eric had gone grey at his temples, and looked terrible. "You need a rest."

"I'm fine, really." he replied. They went back to the room and the doctor was just coming out. "How is she doing?" Eric asked.

"She is doing very well apart from the fact that she doesn't seem able to recognise anything, or speak. Maybe that will come back in time, but at the moment we can't say when or how I'm afraid." he said.

"Thank you," Eric said and the doctor went. They went back in the room and Eric looked at Vicky, who was just looking at him. "It's okay, sweetheart. The doctor said that you are doing well and we have just got to wait," he said as he leaned over to gently kiss her cheek, but Vicky flinched and pulled her head away from him. That was the final straw for Eric. She had never in her life backed away from him or refused him a kiss, and it

147

hurt him like nothing before. He knew then it wasn't his Vicky lying there.

David saw what happened and tried to comfort Eric, but whatever he said was to no avail. Eric held Vicky's hand and kept telling her about the two of them, and about their home and Tom and the pub. David joined in too, telling her all different stories. The following day David went home for a couple of days and said he would be back, but before he went the doctor had come to tell them that they were going to transfer Vicky to a hospital nearer home, where they had a specialist for brain damage cases.

"Brain damage," Eric said.

"Yes, we have to check it out, I'm afraid. Mrs Armstrong isn't responding to anything, so we have got to check for the obvious. I will make the arrangements and let you know."

Eric sat down, completely winded. "Brain damage. Vicky can't be brain damaged. Can she?" he said with tears in his eyes, looking at David. David didn't know what to say. His brother was distraught.

* * *

The transfer went well. It had been three weeks now since Vicky woke up, and she still hadn't said anything. Everybody had been to see her but she hadn't spoken to anyone, just looked at them. Eric had tried a couple of more times to kiss her cheek but got the same response as before: she backed away from him and it crucified him, and David and his mom and dad could see that it was slowly killing him, that he had lost his true love.

One afternoon when Eric was sitting talking to her, trying to get her to remember things, she started looking round the room. Eric noticed her eyes going from one thing to another, then they rested upon him and she smiled.

"Where am I, Eric?" she suddenly said, looking at him.

Eric's heart skipped a beat. "Vicky," he said.

She was still looking at him. "What's going on?" she asked.

He got up, leaned over her and kissed her cheek. No flinch, no rejection; it felt wonderful. "You're in hospital, sweetheart, you had to have an operation," he told her, and got up to get the nurse. She came in and did some more checks, asking Vicky questions all the time, and she was answering them. When she had gone, after telling them that the doctor would be round sometime soon to see them, Eric sat by the bed and held Vicky's hand.

"What happened, Eric?" she asked, looking at him. He relayed everything, then stopped and looked at her. She frowned as she looked at him.

"What's the matter?" he asked.

"I don't remember you having silver streaks in your hair," she said, looking at him.

"No, I hadn't," he said, elated that she could remember. And she pulled his hand up to her mouth and kissed it. That was when Eric knew he had got his Vicky back; his one true love was back with him. He thanked the Lord and everybody and everything.

Christmas was coming and Vicky was still in hospital, but doing very well. She might even be released for the New Year. When the doctor came round, he told them that she could go home the day before New Year's Eve.

"Thank you," was all Eric could say; he was elated. The preparations were made and on the morning, Vicky had a private ambulance to take her home. Everybody was there and welcomed her home. Eric was unbelievably happy to have his wife back with him and home again. He had never loved her so much in his life. The year 2000 had arrived and they all saw in a new year and a new millennium that they might not have been celebrating with such zest.

"I'm okay, sweetheart, really," she told him, looking up at him from the chair as he looked down at her.

"I know you're getting there, but it's hard seeing you so ill," he said as he knelt down next to her and kissed her. She put

149

her hand up to his face and traced his scar with her fingers. He looked so tired.

"Please go and get yourself a drink and unwind a bit, I'm worried about you. You look so tired," she said to him quietly.

"If it makes you happy I will," he said, and kissed her as he got up. She sat there for a while, just watching everybody. She was feeling tired, and her head ached. Eric and David were watching her from across the room.

"How has she been?" David asked him, concerned.

"She seems all right but she gets tired really easy, and I think that's what's up now," he said, looking at her. He went back over to her. "Do you want to go up to bed?" he asked her.

"Yes, I think I do, if you don't mind."

"As long as you are okay, then I don't mind anything. Come on, I'll take you up," he said as he helped her up off the seat. She said her good nights to everyone and they all kissed her, and Dolly gave her one of her hugs.

"Sweet dreams, angel," Tony said to her as he kissed her cheek and smiled at her. They made their way upstairs and Eric helped her get ready for bed. She looked up at him and started crying, burying her head in his chest.

"Hey, what's the matter," he asked as he folded his arms round her.

"You have had a really rough time the last few weeks and I'm worried about you, you look done in, you need a rest," she told him through her tears.

"I'm fine sweetheart, really, if I wasn't I would say, because I'm not leaving your side, okay?" he said as he bent his head down and kissed her tears away.

She ran her fingers through his hair and smiled at him. "You would say, wouldn't you. Mind, you look rather distinguished with your new silver streaks I've given you," she said.

He laughed. "You're worth every one I've got. Now come on, into bed with you." He made sure she was okay and she told him to go back down, but he wouldn't. He got into bed next to her and she lay wrapped in his arms, and that's how they fell to sleep.

January passed and every day Vicky got a little better. Her hair had started growing again and she was eating properly now, which was helping her too. Eric had taken a couple of months away from any work so he could be with her, and they relished their time together. With Vicky wrapped up they went out for drives, or they sat wrapped around each other on the settee. Every day got better and Eric could see a big improvement in her. February rolled into March and she was up and about, though only moderately.

Eric had started to go in to work for one day, just to check over things. She missed him so much when he did, but there was always someone to take his place so she was never lonely. Tom came to see her every night after school; he was brilliant and he loved her to bits. They had grown really close and spent a lot of time together. He was growing up fast. The beginning of May was here and Vicky was finally discharged from the hospital, after having to go back for regular check-ups. She was now back in good health, and she felt great.

Eric hugged her when they came out of the hospital. He had been to every check-up with her. She looked up at him and kissed him there and then on the car park. "I love you so very much, Eric Armstrong," she said as she touched his face with her fingertips.

"I love you too, Vicky," he said and had tears in his eyes.

"My turn to wipe away the tears," she whispered.

"I really thought I'd lost you this time sweetheart, it's such a relief to know you're back to one hundred percent again and I've got my sweet loving Vicky back." And he hugged her tight. They got home and relayed the news that Vicky had been discharged, and spent a bit of time with everyone and waited for Tom to get in from school. Vicky had wanted to see him especially, to tell him herself. They got back in the house about seven-thirty, later than expected but it didn't matter. "I think I will have a

glass of wine to celebrate," Vicky said as she put her arms round
Eric and hugged him. They sat watching TV, and around eleven
o'clock decided to go to bed. When they were in the bedroom,
Vicky put her arms round Eric's neck and kissed him.

"Make love to me tonight, for God's sake, Eric," she said as
she kissed him again. It had been seven months since they had
last made love, and now Vicky felt good and she wanted her
man.

"Are you sure you're okay," he said, responding to her kisses.

"Never better. I just want you, and you have been so patient
with me, so tonight's my treat to you because I'm desperate for
you," she said, starting to undo his trousers.

"I have never wanted you so much in my life," he said,
kissing her neck. They were on the bed naked in minutes and
they made love continuously for the next three hours, catching
up for lost time. It was absolute heaven for them both. They
eventually fell to sleep wrapped around each other.

Their fifteenth wedding anniversary in June was special
to them, because they very nearly didn't reach it. It was eight
months now since Vicky's operation, and they decided to finish
the holiday they started in October. Eric booked them on another
cruise for two weeks. "Two weeks of luxury for the woman I
adore," he told her as he kissed her.

She responded to his kisses with tenderness. "Two weeks of
luxury that you deserve," she said as she cupped his face with
her hands and looked into his eyes. "I love you," she told him as
she looked at him.

"I know," he said and held her tight. They went away in time
for their anniversary and had two weeks of sheer bliss. On the
day itself they ordered room service and stayed in bed most of
the day, just wanting to be alone with each other. They made
love, then slept, then made love again; they were totally together.

When they got home everybody said how well they both
looked. Vicky was near enough back to normal; her hair was
growing and she had put some weight back on. The tired look

had left Eric's face and eyes, and he was back on form too. They spent the evening with the family at David's house, and everyone was happy. Lynn and Sarah were making a fuss of Vicky and the kids were all in bed apart from Tom, who wouldn't leave Vicky's side. She told him to go and spend some time with his dad, and that she would be all right. He did just that, and she could see Eric playing him up and laughing. She watched them both and thought that their children would have been fourteen and twelve years old by now, had she not lost them. She shook herself and carried on, watching Eric as Sarah and Lynn chatted about schools and parent groups. Eric looked over and saw her watching him, and winked at her.

She smiled, blew him a kiss and then got up and went into the kitchen. It was a mild summer evening, so she stepped out into the garden and sat on the bench up by the tree, relishing the peace and quiet. She sat watching a squirrel furrowing in the border. She was totally oblivious to anything. Suddenly she could hear shouting coming from the house then realised they were shouting for her.

Eric and David came rushing out of the back door, calling her. She got up and called them. Eric was down the garden like a shot. "We have been looking for you everywhere, sweetheart. Are you all right?" he asked, hugging her to him.

She stepped back and looked up at him, smiling. "I was just sitting here enjoying the peace and quiet, watching him," and she pointed to the squirrel who was now up the tree.

Eric laughed. "Oh, Vicky, you had us all worried. You've been gone half an hour."

"Sorry. I didn't mean to alarm you," she said as she reached up and kissed him.

"It's okay, sweetheart, don't worry," he said as he hugged her to him. And with that, they walked back up to the house and she got told off by everybody.

Tom came and gave her a great big hug. "Don't go away again, Aunty Viddy, will you please," he said, looking at her.

She put her arms round him and hugged him back. "It will take a lot to get rid of me, sunshine," she told him, smiling and kissing the top of his head.

They went back home about eleven. Once they were back in the house, Eric came and wrapped his arms round her. "You scared me tonight." he whispered. She did no more than kiss him. She then took his hand and led him up the stairs. They stood in the bedroom and undressed each other, melting together. He picked her up and gently lay her on the bed. She was hungry for him, he could tell, because he was for her. He started kissing her, working his way down to her breasts and then her stomach, kissing her scars and the parts that drove her crazy. She grabbed at his body, never wanting it to end.

They turned and she was on top of him. Now it was him grabbing at her body. She sat right upon him then and he held her hips tight, entering her again. She leaned backwards, and slid her hands down his legs and up again. They were in unison with each other. Their sweat mingled between them, and they turned and turned until they reached the place they both wanted to be.

***

The months passed by and September came. Vicky may have been one hundred percent again, but it didn't stop Eric keeping an eye on her. They were helping out for the weekend in the pub, as they were short-staffed because of illness. They were quiet for a Saturday night, but quite a few people were on holiday. David and Lynn were in having a drink, so they were chatting between serving. "Have you heard that Jake's niece Cathy has come from Wales to see him?" Lynn said to Vicky.

"Never. I thought she didn't have anything to do with her mother."

"She hasn't come to see her mother, apparently," she said.

"That's nice then for her to come and see Jake," she said as she went to serve someone.

Eric came over and put his arm round her when she had finished. "You okay, sweetheart?" he asked.

"Yes, I'm good thanks," she replied, kissing his cheek.

Just then Jake walked in with his niece. Eric, David and Lynn all had to do a double take. It was like looking at a slightly older version of Vicky. Vicky looked over. Jake came up the bar and Vicky went up to him. He ordered his drinks and beckoned Eric over. "Can you both spare a few minutes tomorrow morning?" he asked them.

Eric looked at Vicky. "Yes, that should be okay. About ten-thirty in here," she said. He nodded and walked over to his niece, who had sat down. They were quietly chatting, but Eric noticed they kept looking over at him and Vicky. "I wonder what that's all about then," Eric said to Vicky as they went back over to David and Lynn.

"Blimey. Did you see her? She's just like you, Vicky. Sure you never had a sister?" David laughed.

"Quite sure, thank you, well, as far as I know anyway," she said as she playfully hit him. But Vicky had noticed the likeness too. Then she remembered what Jake had said before about his sister making her daughter have her baby adopted. She suddenly went pale and queasy and had to sit down, remembering her adoption papers.

Eric was over to her like a shot, and David was up and round the bar. "What's wrong, sweetheart? Tell me," Eric said urgently.

"Can I have some water, please?" she asked.

David got her water and she sipped it. "Vicky, tell me, are you all right?" Eric asked again.

She looked up at him. "I'm fine sweetheart, really, but I think I know why Jake is coming to see us tomorrow," she said.

He looked at her, puzzled. "I will tell you when we have done last orders and he has gone, okay?" she said and went to get up.

"You stay there, Vicky. I will help Eric. Have a chat with Lynn," David said as he went to help.

"Are you sure you're all right?" Lynn asked when both men were busy.

Vicky looked over to them. "Yes, honestly, I'm fine. I just thought I had realised something, but I hope I'm wrong about it," she told her. When everyone had gone and they had locked up, the four of them sat having a last drink. Vicky told them her suspicions, and Eric remembered Jake telling them about his niece.

"That was years ago, though, wasn't it," he said. "Surely you don't think that your her daughter."

Vicky said, looking at David, "Look at the resemblance, and if she was fourteen when she had her baby then I'm the right age. I remember Jake saying it was thirty-one years ago when he told us then, and at the time I was thirty-one. She would be fifty now," she told them. "I hope I'm wrong, I really do," she said as she hugged Eric's arm.

They left the pub just after and walked home arm in arm. Eric tried to put Vicky's mind at rest about it all. They got in the house, and Eric went and poured her a large brandy. "Get this down you; it will help you sleep," he said as he passed it to her and kissed her. They went to bed and just lay in each other's arms. Eric could tell she just wanted to go to sleep, and as long as she was in his arms he wasn't bothered.

The next morning was different, though. Vicky woke and went and made some tea. She took it back upstairs to the bedroom. She stood looking at Eric's muscular body. He was lying across the bed on his back. She loved the very bones of this gentle giant of a man. She gently got back into bed and started kissing his chest, working her way down to his stomach and beyond, feeling him harden at her touch. She felt his hands on her shoulders, and he was aroused as much as she was. She slid back up him and kissed him. He gently rolled over on top of her and they made passionate love to each other, never wanting it to end. They ached for each other.

"No Daddy. You're hurting me. Stop, please. NO!" she screamed. Eric woke with a start, wrapping his arms round her whilst she turned and sobbed into his chest. She hadn't had one of these nightmares for ages.

"It's okay, sweetheart. I'm here, I've got you," he said to her softly, holding her whilst her sobs subsided. They had fallen back to sleep spooned together.

She pulled back a little and looked up at him. "Thank you," she said as she gently kissed him. He hugged her to him, not having to say a word, and they just lay there. He looked over at the clock, remembering that Jake was coming to the pub at ten-thirty. It was now nearly ten o'clock.

"Vicky," he whispered in her ear, kissing her cheek. She turned her head up to him sleepily and looked into his eyes. "It's nearly ten o'clock, sweetheart and you told Jake we would see him at half past."

Vicky groaned and buried her head back into his chest, and snuggled back up to him. "I know I did. But I want to stay here with you," she said, kissing his chest and stroking it with her fingertips.

"Well, we can always come back later," he said playfully.

She looked up at him. "Can I hold you to that?" she smiled.

"You most definitely can, because you're driving me mad doing what you're doing at the moment," he said as he made himself get up and pulled her with him, groaning.

They were at the pub just before half ten, and started to sort things out. Their manager Brian was back in today, so they hadn't got too much to do. There was a knock on the door, and Eric went and opened it. Jake came in by himself. Vicky made them some coffee and they sat down.

"I'm sorry about this, but I have something to tell you and ask you," he said. Eric caught hold of Vicky's hand and squeezed it.

"Go on, Jake, we're listening," Vicky said.

"Well, to start with, do you remember about four or five years ago, I told you of my sister who sent her daughter away to have a baby at fourteen?"

"Yes, we remember it well, Jake," Vicky said, and she told him all what they remembered.

"Well, my sister died last week, God help her, and her daughter Cathy has come back for a bit to try and help sort things out. She has come back for two reasons. One is to see her mom buried, because she is relieved she's gone. And two is to see her daughter, if she will see her," he said, looking at them.

"We're sorry about your sister, Jake; we hadn't heard. But what has it got to do with us?" Eric asked.

"I didn't think she knew where she was," Vicky said, looking at Jake.

"She didn't. But I do. I have known since the day she was born where she was, but had promised my sister never to tell. But that promise doesn't exist now she's gone, and I know Cathy has always wanted to see her. I have never been able to say anything until now," he told them as he sipped his coffee. "Well, what I have got to say might shock you. But I am not saying it with malice, believe me," he said.

"Go on, we're listening," Vicky said softly, and she felt Eric's hand tighten round hers.

"Well, the daughter she had was you, Vicky. And your dad adopted you because he and your mom couldn't have children," he said and looked at them both sadly.

Eric felt Vicky's hand tighten in his, and he looked at her. She had gone pale but just sat there, dumbstruck. "You mean all those years you saw Vicky growing up you knew who she really was?" Eric asked.

"Yes, but I couldn't say anything because my sister and your dad, Vicky, asked me not to."

"Stop calling him my dad. Because he isn't, is he, he was a bastard to me after my so-called mom died and I suffered years of hell, hell and abuse you wouldn't know nothing about. I don't want to know. Not now. When the bastard died I found out I was adopted because I found the papers. If I had wanted to know I would have sorted it out myself then, because her name is on the adoption papers," she said. Eric looked at her again; he could see she was hurting big time.

"Would you see her, Cathy, your mom? Vicky, please," Jake asked.

"No, I don't want to. I have my life and it's a good one. We've worked hard. I don't need anyone else in it," she told him.

"She wants to see you, though," he said sadly.

"Well, she saw me last night, didn't she?" she snapped at him.

"I think you had better leave, Jake," Eric said as he got up and motioned him towards the door.

"I'm sorry," Jake said as he went.

"As you may be, Jake, but I'm not having Vicky upset and at the moment she is so leave it, okay?" Eric said to him, and closed the door. He went back over to Vicky and she had got her elbows on the table with her head in her hands, sobbing.

He gently pulled her up to him and stood holding her. "What have I done to deserve so much bad luck in my life? All I have ever wanted is to love you. But I have had everything else thrown at me too. I've lost two babies and nearly died, and then not had the chance to have any more thanks to that bastard. I was nearly killed by a crazy sister-in-law and that ended up with me having a bloody brain tumour and nearly dying all over again. I was beat and whipped to oblivion by a bastard that wasn't anything to do with me after all. And now I find out my real mom was only fourteen when she had me, my nan was a stuck-up cow and, to top it all, my great uncle knew all along."

She looked up at him and could see him starting to smile, and they both burst out laughing. "It doesn't sound so bad when you put it like that, really, does it?" Eric said smiling, and kissed her. "Oh Vicky, I do love you. And whatever you decide to do I am one hundred percent behind you, okay? But I don't need to tell you that, do I, because you already know," he said, looking down at her.

"Why do I deserve you? You have got to be the most loving, adorable, understanding man I have ever known. You always manage to lighten things and see the funny side of things, make me laugh and cheer me up. And you have been there for me forever, haven't you, every time. I love you so much, Eric; I just hope you realise how much," she said.

"I do know, yes. You came back from the brink of death to stay with me, and every time my love for you grew even stronger," he said and they kissed, a longing loving kiss that said everything to each other. They went home not long after, and sat and talked about what Jake had told them. Vicky still couldn't get her head round what she had been told. The dad she knew wasn't her dad, just a demented bastard. So who was? She now had a mom again after all these years who suddenly wanted to know her, but she didn't want to know her. It was strange. But she knew one thing for sure. She loved Eric more than anyone or anything. He was her world and nothing or no one else came close or ever would.

***

A few days went by and they saw nothing of Jake. Eric watched as Vicky slowly tortured herself, trying to think what to do. So far in her life, apart from him, she had had all the bad luck she could handle and he wasn't going to stand by and see her possibly get hurt by a woman she didn't know. They were in the kitchen at home and Vicky was keeping herself busy with everyday things. Eric was sitting reading the paper, looking up over it at her. She saw him watching her.

"Why don't you come over here and give me a kiss," he said, and folded away his paper. She smiled at him, came over and sat on his lap, wrapped her arms around his neck and promptly kissed him. "You taste good," he said as he kissed her neck.

"If I didn't know you better, I would say you are after misbehaving, Mr Armstrong," she said as she played with his shirt buttons. His hand slipped inside her blouse and she held him close to her. They kissed again, and the buttons started to come undone. She could feel the hardening of him against her as they gave in to each other.

Suddenly, the doorbell rang. "Oh, bloody hell no," Eric gasped against Vicky's breasts.

"Leave it," she told him, pulling him back to her urgently. Their hands were all over each other. The doorbell went again. "For fuck's sake, not now," he said, gasping.

"You can't stop now, Eric, leave it," she said, her breath hot on his face.

"We've got to go. It might be important," he said as they struggled to get up and tried to compose themselves. "Later," he whispered to her as he turned to go and answer the door, cursing. He opened the door and Jake stood there. "Hello Jake, what's up?" Eric asked, rather shortly.

"Oh, hello Eric. I was wondering if I could have a word with Vicky," he asked. Eric beckoned him in. They went into the kitchen where Vicky was putting the kettle on. Jake seemed really nervous.

"What is it then, Jake," Eric asked again, looking over at Vicky.

"Cathy wants to know if you will see her before she goes home," he said to Vicky. Eric was still looking at Vicky, and saw her blanch and grab the edge of the worktop. He was over to her in a shot.

"Jake, just go, okay. We will let you know," he said as he got Vicky onto a chair. With Jake gone Eric sat with Vicky, holding her hand. "You okay now?" he asked.

She looked up at him. "What shall I do?" she asked him.

"That's entirely up to you, sweetheart. Whatever you decide I'll support you okay.."

She sat there and suddenly decided what she wanted. "I'll see her," she suddenly said. "Because if I don't then I will never know what she is like, will I, and all I will do is wonder what if," she said, looking at him.

"As long as you're sure. Do you want me to let him know and arrange for you to see her somewhere quiet?" he asked.

"Yes, let him know please, but I want to see her here and I most definitely want you with me," she said, squeezing his hand.

"That's okay, sweetheart. I'd got no intention of leaving you on your own anyway." He smiled at her.

She leaned over and kissed him. "Thank you," she whispered.

It was arranged that Cathy and Jake would come on Thursday evening. Cathy was going home on Saturday. It was nearly eight o'clock and Vicky was pacing the floor. Eric went up to her and pulled her to him. "Hey, you're wearing the carpet out," he laughed, and kissed her.

"I'm dreading this," she whispered as she put her head against his shoulder. The bell rang. "Oh God," she said and Eric squeezed her, then went to answer the door.

They followed Eric back into the living room. "Hello Vicky," Jake said, and turned to Cathy. "This is Cathy."

They both nodded at each other. "I'm grateful that you agreed to see me," Cathy said as she sat down.

"Well it has been a shock to find all this out, but everyone has to have a chance," Vicky replied.

"You have grown up lovely, I will say that much," Cathy said, looking at her.

"Thank you."

"Jake says that you have been married for nearly sixteen years."

"Yes, sixteen years next June. And this is my husband Eric," Vicky said, taking Eric's hand.

"Pleased to meet you, Eric," she said.

"You too," he replied, keeping hold of Vicky's hand. They made small talk, then she started asking Vicky about her upbringing and her parents.

"I tried to keep you," she suddenly said, "but back then it wasn't heard of for a girl to have a baby out of wedlock, especially one as young as I was, and my mother was evil to me, she beat me with a stick when she found out I was pregnant. Before she sent me away to have you, before I was showing any signs. By the time I went to live with my aunty I hated her. And when she told me, yes told me, that you were being adopted I screamed at her like a banshee, but she slapped me and told me to grow up. She was a wicked, evil woman. Sorry, Jake," she said, looking over at him.

"It's okay, Cathy, I never agreed with what she done anyway, did I?" he said.

Cathy looked over at Jake and smiled. "No, you never have, have you."

"Who is my father then?" Vicky asked.

Cathy looked down to the floor. "I can't remember his name," she said.

Eric didn't believe her; he saw the way she looked when asked.

"Was he the same age as you?" Vicky said. She was getting fed up, because all Cathy wanted to do was talk about herself.

"Yes, he was," she replied. She was lying again; Eric was watching her. Why was she lying about Vicky's father? Why didn't she just tell her the truth? She had the right to know. "Anyway, it's me that wants to get to know you, not him," Cathy said.

"Did he ever know that you were pregnant, or was he not told and has never knew?" Vicky asked.

Cathy looked down at the floor again. "Does it really matter about him? I want to know if I can start seeing you regular and get to know you better," she said, looking over at Eric, then back to Vicky.

"I will see you again on one condition," Vicky said, looking at Eric.

"What's that?" Cathy asked.

"That you start telling me the truth about my father as well," she said.

"What do you mean?" Cathy said, sounding shocked.

"Well, so far you have told me all about yourself, but for some reason you are lying about my real father. Why?"

"I'm not lying at all. I can't remember his name," she said, looking down at her hands this time.

"Fine. I will see you again, but if you can't remember anything about my father I won't see you again after that," Vicky told her.

"What's so fascinating about your father when it's me that has asked to see you and get to know you?"

"Well, I have got two parents, haven't I? And I would like to see him too, if I'm going to do this at all," Vicky said as she got up. "It's late. We can arrange to meet again when you come back if you want." Eric got up and moved into the hall. "I'm sorry if I'm not the daughter you expected me to be, but I suffered big time when I was growing up, and now I have a good life and a loving husband and I won't have it messed up by anybody. I have nothing to lose by wanting the truth, have I?" Vicky said as she moved towards the front door.

"Yes, well, I go back tomorrow but I will be back Monday," she told them.

"Monday! What about your husband and the farm? Doesn't he need you there?" Jake asked, surprised.

"No, he will be all right, he always is," she said.

Eric looked at her and frowned. Vicky saw the look on his face. The door closed behind them.

"What's wrong?" Vicky asked Eric.

"I don't know really, I can't put my finger on it. But she's lying about a lot of things, I'm sure of it," he said, putting his arms round her.

"I'm sure she's lying about my real father, but I can't understand why," she said, putting her head on his shoulder.

"I'm not going to have you upset, Vicky, no matter what," he told her.

"I know and I won't let it upset me, honest," she said as she looked up at him.. "Thank you for just being you and being here for me." She reached up and kissed him.

"I love you more than anything, Vicky, where else would I be?" he said as he returned her kiss.

"I love you too," she whispered.

The weekend passed and Monday morning came. "What are you going to do when Cathy comes back?" Eric asked Vicky as they got ready for work.

"I don't know, really. But I hope she will be able to tell me something about my real father," she said, looking at him through the mirror. She sat and watched him as he got dressed. This man had been here for her through thick and thin, and she couldn't express just how much she loved him.

He saw her watching him. "Don't you get getting any ideas sitting there, young lady," he said, smiling at her. "I know what's going through your mind. I can see by the look on your face," he continued as he buttoned his shirt.

She got up and went over to him. "Now that was a waste of time, wasn't it," she said as she put her arms round him.

"What was?" he asked, looking down at her.

"Buttoning your shirt," she said as she started to unbutton it.

"You are terrible to me, do you know that? You use and abuse me," he said as he responded to her.

She could feel him hardening already through his trousers, and it excited her even more. "I'm going to be late for work at this rate; you really are a bad influence on me, Vicky Armstrong," he said as he kissed her.

"Are you complaining?" she asked seductively as she undid his trousers and slipped her hand in.

He gasped with delight. "No, and I never would. But at this moment you're killing me. Let me at you," he said as he gently pushed her onto the bed. Within minutes they were seducing each other, and not long after the height of their passion erupted and they lay there breathless for a while.

Eric got up and pulled her up off the bed. "Can I go to work now?" he asked as he kissed her again, smiling.

"I suppose so," she said teasingly. She kissed his cheek and went back over to the mirror.

"I will see you lunchtime and you had better not have changed your mood," he said, laughing as he came over and kissed her.

"Tease," she said, blowing him a kiss as he walked out of the room.

Lunchtime came and Jake turned up with Cathy. "I wasn't expecting you so soon," Vicky said as she opened the door.

"Cathy has something to tell you," Jake said as they walked into the living room.

"Oh yes, what's that then?" Vicky asked.

"I can't tell you about your real dad," she said.

"Why not?"

"Because he has other kids," she told her.

"So that means I have half-brothers and sisters," Vicky said.

"Yes, you have two half-brothers." Cathy told her.

"Well, why won't you tell me about them?" Vicky said, getting rather infuriated.

"Just tell the poor girl, Cathy," Jake said.

"No. it's got nothing to do with you anyway," she said to Jake.

"Oh, but it has, hasn't it?" he told her.

"Well, okay, but you probably won't like it," she said, taking a deep breath. "Your father is your uncle," she blurted out.

Vicky sat there, astounded. "You mean my real dad is your own brother Peter?" she asked.

"Yes he is, and he knows you exist but doesn't know you are his," she said.

"So you and him were..." Vicky couldn't even say it. "God, you are disgusting, your own brother, that's incest!"

"Yes, that's right, it is, but I loved him more than a brother," Cathy replied.

"Is that why your mother disowned you, because she knew what you had done with your own brother?" Vicky asked.

"Probably, but I never forgave her for taking Peter away from me or for taking you off me."

"She did it for the best, obviously," Vicky said, shocked and still unable to take it all in.

Just then, Eric came in. He took one look at Vicky and knew something was wrong. "What's going on?" he asked.

"Cathy and Jake are just leaving," Vicky said as she got up.

Jake was really quiet. He looked ashamed of his niece. "I'm sorry, Vicky. I didn't know until this morning," he said quietly as they went out.

"Know what!" Eric asked, looking puzzled.

Vicky put her hand on his arm and looked up at him. He could see the anguish in her eyes and didn't say anything else. "You will see me again won't you?" Cathy asked as she went out.

"I don't know," was all Vicky could muster up to say. The door closed behind them and Vicky collapsed into Eric, wrapping her arms round him. "I'm so glad I have you," she said as she held him.

"You've got me forever," he said as he put his arms round her. "What's going on, sweetheart?" he asked as he held her out from him and looked down at her.

"I think you had better sit down and I will tell you everything," she said as they went into the living room.

Half an hour later Eric was the one who was astounded. "My God, Vicky, that's disgusting," he said.

"That's exactly what I called her," she told him.

"What will you do? Will you see her again?" he asked.

"If I do it will only be to find out the full story about my real dad, Peter. I don't really want to know her. There's something not quite right about her somewhere along the line, and I can't figure out what it is," she said, looking at him.

"Well, you know I'm here for you whatever you decide, okay?" he said as he kissed her and held her close.

167

"Aren't you always? That's why I love you so much," she said as she put her head on his shoulder.

A week passed and Vicky hadn't heard anything off Cathy or Jake. She tried to carry on as normal but something about Cathy was niggling her, and she couldn't grasp what it was. It was now October, and everywhere was starting to gear up for Christmas. "Shall we have a big family Christmas in the house this year?" Vicky said one morning as they lay snuggled up in bed.

Eric looked down at her. "You, sweetheart, can have anything you want," he said and kissed her.

She looked him in the eyes and gently stroked his scarred cheek, then kissed it. "You spoil me, do you know that?" she said softly.

"Yes, I know I do and you are worth everything you have, because I love you," he said.

"I love you too, more than anything."

"I know you do," and with that they kissed longingly. They gently caressed, arousing each other's passions. Eric slid on top of her and entered her gently and slowly. He wanted to feel every inch of her. They made love with so much feeling for each other, their hearts ached. Vicky didn't want him to stop. Ever.

CHAPTER NINE

The end of October was here, and Jake came to see Vicky. It was Saturday lunch time, and she and Eric were in the house. "I was wondering when I would next hear anything off her," Vicky said.

"I'm afraid you won't see her again, Vicky," Jake said sadly as he sat down.

"Oh. Why, what's happened?" she asked.

"Well, it's a long story and if you've got the time, I would like to tell you it all. That's why you haven't seen me, because I have been finding out the truth for you because I think you deserve it," he said as he sat down.

"Right. Thank you, Jake. We're listening," she said as she sat down next to Eric on the sofa and he took her hand, squeezing it.

"Well, I will start right at the beginning from when you were born, because now I know the whole truth I'm ashamed to call her my niece. She is a disgrace to the family," he said, looking at them.

"Don't worry, Jake, I'm sure Vicky won't blame you for anything, will you, sweetheart?" Eric said, looking at her and squeezing her hand again.

"No, I won't. None of this is your fault, Jake. Please, carry on."

"Thank you Vicky," he said as he tried to compose himself. "Well, when my sister told me that Cathy was pregnant, I presumed it was by some boy she had been with. Anyway, it was arranged that she would go and stay with an aunt of ours in Wales. Because Peter was two years older than her he had to be told the reason why she was going, but was threatened by his mother not to say anything to anyone, and was told that the father was a boy Cathy had met at some youth club. So when the time came, and I think she was about four months gone with you and just starting to show, she was sent to Wales. Before you were born I had spoken to your so-called dad because I knew how desperate your mom was for a baby. They agreed to adopt you legally but Cathy was never to know, as it was too close to home. Everything went through no trouble and you were brought up as their own and never told, as your dad wanted you to remain his until the day he died. Even more so after your mom died. And you did." Vicky shuddered at that thought, and Eric clasped her hands tight in his. "Everything went well and Cathy remained in Wales, as she couldn't forgive her mom for taking you off her and, as I found out recently, taking her away from Peter too, who she had an abnormal love for. The years went by, but once a year I would go and see Cathy and when she reached twenty-five she married Owen, a farmer, and lived and worked on his farm. She seemed happy enough, but they really struggled and never had much money, and underneath she began to resent everybody and I think that is what finally turned her so nasty. I always knew who you really were and watched you grow up and flourish into the wonderful woman you are today, even after the rotten start you had. When her mom died, Cathy decided to come home because she wanted to make sure she was really gone. That was when she told me she wanted to find you, to see if you would see her. So I told her after much deliberating where you were, and she asked me to come and see you as I did. Well, after you had met the first time she began to ask me about your inheritance off your dad, the pub and your businesses, and kept asking me if you were well off. Especially after she had been here and seen what a lovely home you have. I never told her much because it's nothing to do with anybody, and you have both worked hard for what you have today."

"Sorry to butt in, Jake, but would you like some coffee?" Vicky asked as she got up.

"Yes, that would be nice, thank you." She went into the kitchen and began to sort out the coffee things. Eric came in and put his arms round her.

"You okay, sweetheart?" he asked.

She looked up at him and smiled. "I'm fine, really," she said, and kissed him. They took the coffees in and made some small talk, then Jake started again.

"Anyway, the last few weeks, as I told you, I have been trying to find out the truth about things for you, and I finally have. I phoned Owen up myself and asked him what was going on, and he told me that they split up six months ago because she had told him that she had never loved him really, and that she wanted a better life than being a farmer's wife and never having any money, after nearly twenty-five years, I ask you. And then when she came here and found out about you she started to hatch a plan in her head. She did go back to Wales that one weekend when she said she did, and Owen told me that she went to see him and told him that she was going to get what she is owed out of her daughter because she is her real mom and is entitled to it. She could at last live the life she wanted on your money." Jake looked over at Vicky, to see her with tears running down her cheeks. "I'm sorry, Vicky, do you want me to stop?" he asked.

Eric looked at his wife and saw her tears, and immediately felt like he wanted to throttle bloody Cathy for upsetting her. "No, please go on Jake, I need to hear it," she said as Eric put his arm round her.

"You okay?" he whispered. She just looked at him and nodded her head.

"Well, after Owen had told me this I saw Cathy in a different light. She was just a money grabber but I never told her I had spoken to Owen, and I just carried on as normal, but every now and then I would bring up the subject of money to see if she would say anything, and finally she let it slip. That was when she told me about Peter too. I couldn't believe it. I knew you wanted to know who your dad was so I made a deal with her

171

that I wouldn't stick to, but she didn't know that. I told her if she told you about Peter then I would help her get some money off you to live on and have the life she wanted. That's when she came to see you and told you. After that I told her that there was no way I would even consider doing what she wanted, and I told her I had spoken to Owen, that she had been found out in her lie. She went mad and called me all the names under the sun, said I was just like her mom. Anyway, after that I phoned Peter up and explained to him that I needed to see him, but it would have to be face to face. I went over to Ireland to see him, and it was then that I found out some more truths. After I got there, we sat down in his living room and he told me why he went there and about his family.

"I hadn't seen or heard off him for three years, and had a lot of catching up to do. He told me that his mom treated him like dirt after Cathy went to Wales, but he could never understand why. When he reached eighteen he got a job and an apprenticeship, and one of the conditions was that he move to Ireland. He jumped at the chance because he was fed up of his mom hitting him all the time. She had been doing it for two years and it was getting worse, so he went and never came back. I asked him about him and Cathy, and he told me that it only happened the once and she had enticed him into it but he felt dirty afterwards and couldn't even stand to look at her, but she kept trying to touch him all the time and he hated it. He was glad when she went to Wales. Then I dropped the bombshell about you to him. He hadn't got a clue; he was devastated that he had never been told about you. I explained to him that I had only just found out and that his mom had taken the secret to her grave with her, and if his sister hadn't been so greedy for money we would never have found out. He is now fifty-two, has two sons who are your half-brothers, Liam is twenty-six and Keiran twenty-eight, neither of them are married but they are good sons to their dad. His wife Sinead died two years ago from breast cancer. He wants to know if he can come over and meet you, but said he would understand if you didn't want to and not to be worried about upsetting him if you don't," he told Vicky, who was sitting there amazed by what she had heard.

"My God, Jake. You have worked wonders. Thank you," Vicky said as she got up and went over and hugged him.

"Would you like another drink, Jake?" Eric asked, getting up.

"Yes, thank you, and you are worth it, Vicky. I suppose in some way we are related and that makes you even more worth it, and your dad is a fine man," he said.

Eric went into the kitchen to make some more coffee. Vicky came in and put her arms round him. "You okay?" he asked her.

"I don't really know. I think I am, but when I'm with you I'm always okay," she said, looking up at him and kissing him.

He held her tight and then kissed her too. "Are you going to meet your dad?" he asked her.

"I think I will. He sounds genuine, not like his sister. I said there was something about her that I couldn't quite get to grips with, didn't I?" she said, looking at him.

He smiled at her. "Woman's intuition, is it?" he said, smiling down at her.

She laughed, kissed him and went back into the living room. Eric followed her with the coffees. They carried on talking some more while they drank their coffee, and Jake said that he would leave them to think things over.

"I will be in touch within a couple of days," Vicky told him as he left. That night they went to see Tony and Dolly and told David to be there too, as he had always been there for everything. They sat and told them the whole story, and they couldn't believe it.

"Are you going to see your dad, Vicky?" Tony asked her.

"I think I might. He seems really genuine and Jake has said that he is a really nice bloke. Quiet and unassuming," she told them. That night when they got back home, they sat cuddled up on the sofa and drank two bottles of wine.

"If you want to see your dad, just do it," Eric said to her, holding her close to him.

She turned in his arms to face him and looked up at him. "I know this is worrying you, isn't it. Why?" she asked as she kissed his cheek.

"I don't know really, probably because it will mean you having three new men in your life and I will have to share you," he told her as he pushed her hair off her face.

"You are daft sometimes, Eric Armstrong. Nobody, no matter who, would ever come close to you in my life," she said.

He smiled at her and kissed her with a longing. "Do your thing to me, Vic. I can't have you lying on top of me like this. We might have been married nearly sixteen years, but you drive me crazy," he whispered as he kissed her neck. She only had to hear him call her Vic and she knew that he was burning for her again, and she wanted him. She started seductively undressing him, kissing him all the time. His hands were all over her, pulling at her clothes. He rolled off the sofa onto the floor, pulling her down on top of him. She finished undressing him and sat upon him, kissing every part of his body and making him crazy for her.

"Take me now, Vic, for God's sake," he gasped. His breath was hot and fast on her breasts. She slid onto him and they become one as he held her hips, their bodies in rhythm with each other. They rolled about the floor in every position you could imagine.

"Don't ever stop," she panted as he took her again. They were oblivious to everything apart from each other. With everything spent they rolled over, entwined in each other, breathless.

Christmas was nearly upon them, and they had arranged with Jake for her dad and brothers to come over for Christmas, as they were having their family Christmas they had talked about. Vicky was nervous as hell about meeting them. "I've told your dad all about Eric and most things about you, but I have left some gaps for you to fill in," Jake told them one night when he came round.

"Has Cathy definitely gone?" Vicky asked.

"Oh yes, Owen said that she had tried to go back to him but he told her to bugger off," he laughed. They arranged for their first meeting in the pub so everyone could meet the three of them, and it wouldn't be so formal. The day arrived and Vicky was at odds with herself.

Eric could see what she was like, and went up to her and wrapped his strong arms around her. "You will be fine. I'm here for you if you need me; just remember that, okay?" he said as he kissed her.

She looked up at him. "You have always been here for me," she said and held him close, clinging to him for reassurance. Lunchtime came and they went down the Thistle into the back room that had been kept just for them, and waited. They didn't have to wait long before everyone was there, then all that was left was for Jake to arrive with the three people she found herself longing to meet. They walked in just after, and Vicky knew her dad straight away. He had a kind face and was tall and dark. Liam and Keiran followed him, and they were just like him. Jake introduced them all and Peter and Vicky just stood looking at each other. He then opened his arms to her and she went into them gladly. They both cried and clung to each other. When they finally parted she hugged the two lads, then introduced Eric to her dad.

"I'm pleased to meet you at last," Peter said as he shook Eric's hand. Eric took to him straight away. "I hear you take exceedingly good care of my daughter. And you don't know how strange it is to call someone my daughter," he continued.

"Yes, I love Vicky more than anything," Eric told him.

"My, you're a big bloke, I will say that for you," Peter said as he looked Eric up and down. Eric laughed and Vicky came over and he put his arm round her. They all got to know each other, and lunchtime went into evening. They ordered some food and Vicky filled in the gaps Jake had left to her dad. He couldn't believe how well they had done, and told her he was proud of her.

Vicky sat talking to her two brothers for a while, and they hit it off well. Peter was with Dolly and Tony; Eric was stood talking to David. He looked over towards Vicky; he could see that she was happy and it made him feel good. She looked up and he winked at her, and she gave him one of her gorgeous smiles and blew him a kiss. This was noticed by Peter, and it was then that he could tell just how much they thought of each other.

"You will get used to those two," Tony told him, laughing.

"What do you mean?" he asked.

"They are like that all the time. Like a couple of love-struck teenagers even though they've been married nearly sixteen years. They're a great couple, even though I say it myself. But they have come through so much together. That's what we think has made their love for each other so strong. They're inseparable," Dolly told him with a tear in her eye.

Peter could tell there was a special bond between them and he found himself loving his daughter himself already, even though he still hardly knew her. He was yet to find out more about them both. The evening went really well, and everyone had got on great. David and Lynn left and told Peter to make sure that he came over with Vicky and Eric, to meet the kids. Tom wanted to meet him because he had said it would be like having another granddad. Peter laughed at this, not realising the bond his daughter had with Tom. Dolly and Tony left, saying they would see them tomorrow. Finally, Jake went with Liam and Keiran, saying he would see Peter when he got home.

It was nine o'clock and Eric, Vicky and Peter all retreated to the bar, where they sat and had a drink and chatted some more. Peter told them all about himself and about his dead wife Sinead, and more about their two sons. He really was a genuine bloke. They walked back home having said goodnight and left Peter heading towards Jake's, saying they would see him tomorrow.

"Well, how do you feel about everything," Eric asked Vicky as they strolled up the road.

"I think they are really nice and would like to get to know them better, don't you," she answered, looking up at him.

"Yes, your dad is a lovely bloke. I think you have made quite an impression on him. Mind, you make an impression on anyone, but that's me saying that and I love you so I would," he said and stopped, pulled her to him and kissed her in the middle of the lamplit street.

"Thank you, sweetheart, for being here for me," she said to him as their lips parted. They hugged and carried on up the drive and into the house. They went into the living room and Eric poured them both a nightcap, and they sat and drank it and talked about the day. Suddenly, Vicky looked at Eric and she wanted him again. She took his hand and led him up the stairs. Neither of them said a word; they didn't have to. In the bedroom Eric let her undress him; he loved it when she did this. His hands found her zip and undid her dress, and it slipped down her body to her feet.

By now Vicky had him naked and he gently pushed her onto the bed, kissing her. He let her hands wander all over his body like silk on his skin; it drove him crazy. She kissed him from head to toe, stopping in certain places longer and driving him insane, making his skin tingle with delight and arousing him big time. He kissed her body all over, finding the spots that drove her mad. By now he was aching for her, and he could tell she was more than ready for him. He slid on top of her and entered her with a passion. She arched her back as she wrapped her legs round him like a snake. He leaned up on his elbows and looked down at her, never stopping, gently sliding in and out of her. Their eyes met and they kissed; the electricity that went through them was like lightning. They were together, and nothing else mattered. The height of their passion grew to its peak and they came together, calling out each other's name. Breathless. They fell to sleep wrapped around each other. Contented.

The following morning Vicky was woken by Eric kissing her all the way up her spine to the nape of her neck. She turned over to him and he kissed her breasts, making her tingle. "God, I love you so much Vicky," he whispered as he slid on top of her and into her. She groaned with pleasure as he tormented her body with his rhythm. She had never known another lover and never wanted to; Eric reached places that she knew no one else could or would ever reach. He was perfect, her gentle giant. Their passion erupted and they lay there breathless again. He turned and pulled her to him, and they lay spooned together. She loved this man so much, she ached for him. "What time did you tell your dad we would see him?" he asked as he kissed her neck.

"Not until lunchtime, about one o'clock. Why?" she asked.

"Oh, no specific reason. I've got to go and pick something up, that's all."

"Well, as long as you're back here on time. You won't be late, will you?"

"I won't don't worry," he said, and with that he got up and pulled her up off the bed.

"You just make sure you are here for me when I get in, okay?" he said and kissed her again, then started getting dressed. Eric kept his word, and was back before midday. Vicky was waiting for him. He came in, and kissed and hugged her. "Right, I'm sorted now and you look wonderful and taste good as always," he said, smiling. "I'll just have a quick shower and I'm good to go," and he ran upstairs. They got to Jake's and they all sat talking. Vicky loved the soft Irish lilt her brothers had, and she found them to be really good fun to be with. Her dad and Eric were watching them.

"She truly is an amazing woman, isn't she?" Peter said.

"Yes, she is. And she has been through so much, so I tend to try and protect her from things, but I love her so much."

"Yes, I can see you do and the best bit is that she loves you just as much," Peter said, looking over at his newly found daughter. "She told me last night about your accident, the babies you lost and the accident she had involving your ex-sister-in-law, and about the beatings she had off that bastard. She said that if she had lost you because of any of it then she would have given up on life altogether, as she would have had nothing without you. Did you know that?"

"She has never actually said it but I know, because I know how she feels because I was exactly the same when she was in hospital. I was so close to losing her. I would never have coped without her, I know that," Eric told him looking over at Vicky. She looked at them both and smiled. Eric's heart nearly burst with love for this woman. He winked at her and she laughed, blowing him a kiss. Peter smiled to himself and shook his head, loving seeing her happy. The day went by and they all got to know each other really well, and all got on great.

Christmas was going to be wonderful. Christmas morning, Eric woke Vicky with a kiss. "Happy Christmas, sweetheart," he said as he pulled her to him.

"Mm, you too," she answered sleepily, and cuddled up to him.

"What time is Mom coming to give you a hand?" he asked.

"Not till about ten because she wants to see the kids," she said as she kissed his chest.

"Well, in that case it gives us nearly two hours to ourselves. I wonder what we can do," he said suggestively as he stroked her back.

"Eric Armstrong, you are terrible," she laughed, looking up at him.

"What do you mean?" he said all innocently.

"I know you. You've got that look about you."

"Well, what are you going to do about it, may I ask?"

"Absolutely nothing," she said, smiling, and curled back up against him.

He did no more than push her onto her back and looked down at her. "So playing hard to get, are we?" he smiled and kissed her.

"I'm trying to but you're too hard to resist. I could never say no to you because I nearly always want you."

"Only nearly always," he said as his hand slid down her body.

"Okay. Always, always. I give in, you're torturing me," she gasped as he touched her.

"Well, I might torture you some more first and make you wait," he said as he kissed her breasts.

She pulled him back to her. "I'll go mad if you do," she said, kissing him and sliding her hands down his body, making him gasp with delight.

"Jesus, Vicky, I couldn't make you wait because I can't wait myself. Let me at you, for God's sake." With that, he was on top of her and they made the most amazing love, passions burning, pumping into each other with greed. They lay there for a while holding each other, then Eric went and made some tea. When he came back up he had a small parcel with him. "For the woman I love and adore," he said to her as he handed it to her and kissed her.

"Thank you, sweetheart. I wasn't expecting this," she said, looking at him. She opened it and tears rolled down her cheeks. It was an antique gold heart-shaped locket, and inside was a picture of them on their wedding day on one side and the other side was engraved *"I have loved you all my life and will love you till it ends."* The back was *engraved*, too. *"You have my heart forever. Eric.x"*

She turned to him and kissed him, and wrapped her arms round his neck. "Thank you; it's gorgeous. I will treasure it always," she said.

"I knew you would like it, because you know I mean every word that's written on there. I know we don't usually get anything for each other because we don't need anything, but I wanted to do this because you give me so much love in return and make me an extremely happy man all of the time. I never want for anything," he said as he kissed her again. He took it off her and placed it round her neck and fastened it. Then he kissed her neck. "I love you," he whispered.

She turned to him. "Oh, Eric, I love you too, more than anything in this world. You make me feel so contented and safe; you are all I will ever need," she said with tears rolling down her cheeks.

"Hey, don't cry," he said as he kissed away her tears.

"I'm crying because I'm so happy," she laughed, hugging him. They held each other for a while, then their hands began to wander again and they ended up making love again before they got up. They did eventually get up, and started preparing for a fabulous day. The dinner was on and Vicky and Dolly were busy in the kitchen. Suddenly, the door burst open and Tom ran in straight to Vicky and wrapped his arms round her waist.

"Happy Christmas, Aunty Viddy," he said.

She laughed and hugged him. "You too, young man," she said, and looked up to see Eric watching her at the door, smiling. He winked at her and disappeared back through it, smiling. Everyone opened their presents off Eric and Vicky. Dolly loved her gold earrings and necklace. Lynn had some earrings, David had a new watch and Tony had some new gold cufflinks. Vicky had been out and brought her dad a gold St Christopher, and had the back engraved. Dad . Love Vicky. He loved it. Liam and Keiran both had new shirts each. Tom had a new bike, and was in his element. With everything opened and all the mess away, dinner was served. The day passed wonderfully and everyone ate themselves to the bursting point. Everyone joined in the games with the kids and they laughed until they thought their sides would split at some of the antics, mostly Eric and David playing up. Night time came and the little ones went to bed. Tom sat with Vicky telling her about his new presents Eric could see how she blossomed when Tom was about, and it made him love her more.

"Will you be here for New Year?" he asked Peter.

"Well, we don't want to outstay our welcome, but it would be lovely."

"Don't talk so daft. You're welcome here any time," he told him.

"I better tell Vicky then that we're staying," Peter said, looking over at her.

"No, don' t. Let it be a surprise for her, because she thinks you're going home the day before, doesn't she?" Eric said quietly.

"Yes, she does. What's happening then?" he asked.

"We're going down the Thistle to the party there, and it would be great for her if you just walk in and surprise her."

"Okay, let's do it then," Peter said, smiling.

The next few days passed in a blur of enjoyment. The day before New Year's Eve Peter and his sons went for lunch with Eric and Vicky before they pretended to go and catch their ferry home. It had been planned with Jake that they would stay for another three days, but it wasn't to get back to Vicky. The end of the meal came and they all got up to go. Outside, Peter went and put his arms round Vicky. "Don't be too long coming back again, will you?" she said to him through a blur of tears.

"I won't. I promise," he said and kissed her cheek. She kissed Liam and Keiran and the three of them got into Jake's car for him to take them to the ferry. They waved and she stood there looking.

Eric put his arms round her and held her. "Don't worry, sweetheart, they will soon be back," he told her. They walked home and spent the rest of the afternoon curled up on the settee.

New Year's Eve was here and they were busy in the pub, helping to sort everything out. They went home about three o'clock and Vicky started to sort her clothes out for the evening. She had brought a new dress that she knew Eric would love, but hadn't shown it him yet. They curled up on the sofa and watched a film, both of them dozing on and off. "I think we had better make a move; it's nearly seven o'clock," Eric said as he untangled himself from Vicky off the sofa.

"I was so comfy then, you spoilsport," she said as he pulled her up.

"Yes, I know, but you better go and get in the shower; you know how long it takes you to get ready," he said, smiling as he kissed her. She went up and Eric followed her. He watched her get undressed and go into the shower, but the thought of her in there got too much for him and he followed her in. He went up behind her and put his arms round her.

"You sneak," she said as she turned to him. He kissed her hard and she could feel him against her, already aroused for her. She held on to him and wound her legs up round his waist and he held her close, entering her with a fury. They were mad for each other and couldn't get enough. They reached their height together, and the love poured through them both. They stayed there for a few minutes, then he gently lowered her, kissing her softly. She put her hand up to his scarred cheek and traced his scar with her finger. They looked into each other's eyes and knew that what they saw was what was in both their hearts.

Eric was shaving as Vicky walked out of the dressing room. He looked at her through the mirror. She was a vision of pure beauty to him. He stopped what he was doing and slowly turned round and just stood looking at her. She looked fantastic. She had put her hair up and had soft dark curls falling round her face and neck. Her dress was exquisite. Red, just her colour; it had a low-cut tight-fitting bodice showing off her cleavage and waist, and fit snugly round her hips and came to an end about four inches above her knees, showing off her long shapely legs. The sleeves were lace with inset red sequins. Her stilettos were red to match, as were her lips, and she had her locket on nestling just above her cleavage.

He fell in love with her all over again, there and then. "Vicky," he said. He couldn't get his breath.

She looked over at him and smiled. "Do you like it?" she whispered.

"I have never seen you look so beautiful," he said. He went over to her and held her tight. "You are going to be playing havoc with me tonight," he said and kissed her gently on her red lips. He held her at arms length and looked at her. "You look gorgeous. I just hope I can control myself tonight because you are already driving me crazy looking like that," he whispered as he pulled her back to him and held her tight.

She felt him harden against her, and was tempted. "I think you had better hold that till later. I'm ready to go and you're not going to mess me up now, Mr Armstrong. But later, I promise you can mess me up all you like," she softly whispered in his ear, then smiled up at him, kissed him longingly and walked across the room. He had to pull his eyes away from her. It was going to be hard, because he kept finding himself looking at her. She was amazing. They walked down the road to the Thistle arm in arm. Eric still couldn't believe just how gorgeous his wife looked tonight. They went into the function room and were met by David up the bar.

"Hey beautiful, you look wonderful," he said to Vicky as he kissed her cheek.

"Thank you," she said. Eric could see a few of the local men looking at him enviously. He had to be the luckiest bloke in the room tonight. He had a beauty on his arm who happened to be his wife, who he knew loved him and only him, and he would be taking her home and taking her to bed with him. He smiled to himself knowing what was in store for him later; he couldn't wait. They said hello to everyone and sat chatting. Vicky was talking to Sarah; Lynn had the kids and had told Sarah to come out for a bit. Eric was over the other side of the room, talking to one of the locals. He looked up to see his gorgeous wife looking at him, and his heart skipped a beat. He winked at her and she gave him one of her gorgeous sexy smiles; her eyes said it all. The night carried on and about nine o'clock, Eric and David made sure Vicky sat with her back to the door. Sarah kept her talking, and in walked her dad.

He went up behind her and put his hands gently over her eyes. "Guess who," he whispered.

She twisted round and couldn't believe it when she saw him. "Dad!." Peter was over the moon. She had called him dad.

He hugged her and she was full of questions of how and why, and he told her and she playfully smacked him and Eric, who stood next to her with his arm round her shoulders. The night had become perfect for her. Her dad was here and her husband was the most wonderful man on earth and she loved every inch of him more than anything. They saw 2002 in with style, the whole pub was alive; it was wonderful. The night was coming to an end; it was one-thirty and last orders had been served and drank. People were starting to leave. Sarah and David had gone and Jake, Peter and the two lads were just leaving. They said their good-nights and Eric and Vicky went too. They walked home talking about the night.

At the front door, Vicky stopped and reached up and kissed Eric longingly. He looked down at her and smiled. Once in the house, the door closed and Eric had got her back to it, kissing her with passion. "I have had to wait a bloody long time tonight to do this, and you have killed me all night, having to see you looking so sexy. Do you realise what you do to me? You drive me crazy," he whispered to her through his kisses. She was already undoing his clothes, and made it quite clear that she wanted him as bad. He picked her up and carried her upstairs, kissing all the way up. They were undressed in seconds, clothes just abandoned on the floor ,and Vicky pulled him onto the bed.

"Love me, Eric, do to me what you do so well," she gasped and pulled him to her.

"You're going to have it all tonight, I promise, because I'm aching for you. Have been all night," he whispered as he slid down her body, gently kissing it all over. They teased each other and toured each other's bodies, turning to every position possible. The time came, and they were both so desperate. Eric entered her again and then they were in rhythm with each other, grabbing at each other's bodies and holding tight, reaching their heights breathlessly and collapsing into each other panting. "Jesus, Vicky, I love you so much," Eric told her as he held her against him, catching his breath.

"I love you too," she whispered. They wrapped themselves round each other and fell to sleep entwined together.

"NO Daddy no. It hurts. Please don't hurt me, Daddy, no please. I'm bleeding Daddy, no, it stings." She screams. "You stupid little bitch, shut your mouth. Fucking little whore, just like your mother." And the whip comes down on her again curling round her small body like a snake.... Vicky woke in a panic and felt arms holding her tight. She realised that the arms are loving ones, and she is safe. "It's okay, sweetheart, I'm here. You're safe," Eric whispered to her. She turned to him and sobbed into his chest and he held her tight, wanting to protect her always. She didn't have many nightmares now, but when she did they wracked her scarred body. "Shush sweetheart, you're okay, I love you," he whispered as he held her.

The months passed. Vicky and Eric had been over to Ireland to see Peter and his family a few times, and they had been over here. They got on great and it was as if they had known each other years.

***

The spring turned to summer and they celebrated their seventeenth wedding anniversary. They didn't have a party this time; they went away for a few days. It was heaven for them both and they were the loved up couple they always were. Eric celebrated his forty-third birthday; Vicky treated him to a romantic weekend away with all the trimmings. He told her after that she had made his birthday really special to him, and the best trimming was her. She had made sure that they weren't disturbed on his actual birthday, and ordered room service for everything. She had brought some really raunchy, sexy underwear just for him. On his birthday morning she woke him up, kissing him and wearing one of his shirts.

"Morning, birthday boy," she whispered, kissing his back with butterfly kisses.

He slowly turned and looked at her. "Mm, morning gorgeous. Why have you got my shirt on?"

She straddled him and sat on him. "It's your birthday present wrapper. And you have got to unwrap your present," she said seductively as she ran her finger down his chest.

"Mm, I could get used to this. Can I start now?" he asked huskily. She could feel him hardening beneath her already.

"You may." He slowly started to undo the buttons from the bottom up, but as he pushed the shirt down over her arms he couldn't believe what he saw. She had on a blood-red lacy Basque complete with suspenders, stockings and garter. It was done up the middle with red lace and her breasts sat firmly in the cups, being pushed up to fullness with her locket nestling in her cleavage. But to top the lot, he noticed that the panties that she had on were only done up with tiny little bows at the side. One flick of his fingers, and they would be off. He was fit to burst.

"Oh fuck, Vicky, I could eat you. You look gorgeous," he said as he ran his hands up and down her, feeling everything about it. She knelt up, releasing the beast from below, and he pulled on the tiny bows and off came the panties. He guided himself into her and she sat on him, looking down at him. "Don't stop, sweetheart, please," he begged, holding her hips. She leaned forward and planted a sweet tender kiss on his lips, feeling him inside her. "God, you taste so good. You're killing me, Vic, don't ever stop being you, please," he said softly as their rhythm started to build pace. They rolled over and over on the bed in every position possible, until neither of them could hold on any longer. They exploded together and collapsed into each other in a heated tangle. They lay there holding each other. "That's the best birthday present I have ever had," he whispered as he held her tight.

"Glad you liked it, sir," she said, smiling up at him.

"Can we have a repeat performance tonight?" he asked.

"Mm, I should think so," she said as she kissed him. That was how the rest of their weekend went, and they went back home completely and utterly loved up more than before, and Eric never forgot it.

***

David and Lynn started having problems, and separated. Tom stayed with David and Davina went to live at Grant and Hilary's with her mom. David saw Davina regularly, though, because there was no animosity between him and Lynn; they just couldn't live together any more. They decided to just live apart. Tom blossomed into a fine young man; he was fifteen now, becoming like Vicky's shadow at everything she did. He idolised her; she had been there for everything for him even through her own troubles.

It was coming up to 2005. Vicky and Eric had been married twenty years. Eric had treated her to a week down on the coast in a private little cabin on a remote part of the hillside. It was heaven. They didn't hardly see anyone all week. They just had each other. Vicky was thirty-nine now, and Eric's forty-sixth birthday was coming up along with Toms sixteenth.

"What do you want to do on your birthday?" Vicky asked Eric one night as they lay on the sofa.

"Surprise me," he said as he pulled her to him and kissed her. "We could do what you did for me when I was forty-three," he said, seductively running his hands down her body.

"Behave," she said, reaching up and kissing him.

"Oh, have I got too," he laughed. She couldn't help it, but she found herself starting to undress him on the sofa. "I thought you said to behave," he whispered as he took off her skimpy panties.

"Mm, I caved in to you as usual. It's what you do to me still." And that was it. They had hot fiery passionate sex on the sofa, not being able to get enough of each other. Over the years their love for one another had never faltered. They were as much in love now as they were twenty years ago when they married.

Vicky looked up at him while they were lying there. "Does that mean I can do anything for your birthday then?" she teased, unbuttoning his shirt again.

"You can do what you're threatening any time," he told her through his kisses. She put her head on his chest and he held her tight. He loved this woman to bits, always had and always will. He could feel her heartbeat against him, and it made him ache for her. "I love you, Vicky," he whispered, and she lifted her head and looked at him.

"I love you too," she said, and kissed him with a kiss that had body and soul in it. They lay there and he felt her undo his trousers, and in slipped her hand.

"Jesus, Vicky," he said as she took his breath away. She kissed him again as she climbed on top of him, and he succumbed to her again. This woman was incredible; she could turn him on in a whisper still, even twenty years down the line. He reached up to her, and she bent and kissed him. Their rhythm increased; they tried hard to hold on but their passion exploded and they fell into each other, exhausted.

THE ENDING

"Will you have one with us, Viddy?" Tom asked her as he got his first round of drinks in now that he was eighteen. All through the years, he had never changed what he called her from a baby. He had told her once that she would always be his Viddy.

"Well, I will have a drink, but I will draw the line at having a pint like these two," she laughed, pointing at Eric and David's drinks. The four of them drank to Tom and Eric, as this was his birthday too' he was forty-eight. They were up the bar, and then they went and joined the rest of the family. The night was golden, and they all parted about midnight. As usual, when Eric and Vicky got home, as soon as the door was shut he had her pinned to it, kissing her.

"Do your thing to me, Vic," he whispered to her, his breath hot on her neck. She succumbed to his touch like she always did, hot for the man she loved so much. Unbuttoning his shirt seductively and working her way down his chest, kissing his body, making him gasp. She undid his trousers and her hand was in there, making him desperate for her. By now he had her clothes off too, and before they knew it they were having hot sex on the stairs, desperate for each others bodies and exploding into a frenzy of passion.

November came and Tom brought home his first "official" girlfriend, as he called her. He had asked his dad if he would mind going to Eric and Vicky's so the three of them could meet her together. He came in with her and introduced everybody, and told them this was Eva. She was a slip of a girl, seventeen, with blonde wavy hair. Tom near enough towered over her, as he was tall and broad like his dad and uncle. It reminded Vicky of when she and Eric were younger; he still towered over her but she loved it that way. He was still her gentle giant, and she loved him more than anything. They all got talking, and found that Eva lived in the village down the far end with her mom and dad. It didn't last, though. which none of them were surprised about, as she turned out to be what Tom called "a slapper." One girlfriend followed another over the months, but Tom got fed up and decided to stick on his own for a bit. He was working now at Armstrong's construction, and he was looking to be a promising bricklayer and plasterer. Eric got him in on some courses, and he was doing well.

"What's involved in the pub business?" he asked his dad one day.

"Why, are you interested in it?" David asked him.

"I don't know, I might be," he answered.

"Talk to Eric and Vicky, too; they know it inside out as well," David told him. He did just that one day and when they told him of the late nights, functions, drunkards and so forth, it put him right off. They all had a laugh over it, though.

Christmas and New Year came, and they saw in 2008 and everything was well. Eric and Vicky were now coming up to their twenty-third wedding anniversary. Nothing had changed between them, though. They still loved each other to bits and still couldn't keep their hands off each other. Even though it wasn't the usual two to three times a day every day, they still made love at least once or twice a day, never missing. They said that that was what had kept them so much in love, their active sex life. Eric was a young, nearly forty-nine-year-old, and still fit and active. Vicky was just forty-two and still had the figure and body Eric loved to touch and explore. Every day he kissed her scars, which had now faded a little but were still there, and every day he drove her crazy doing it. Tom was coming up to his nineteenth birthday and he was now nearly a qualified bricklayer and plasterer, and good at it. Eric had made him, after teaching him what, when and how; he loved it. He still looked upon Vicky as the mom he never had, and cherished her just like his dad and uncle did. He had never laid eyes on his own mother and never wanted to, as his dad and Eric had told him one day just what she had done to Vicky, and had ended up in jail for it. It made him love his Viddy even more. When Tom was there, nobody apart from Eric got a look in with her.

Vicky loved it because she told them that she was loved by three good-looking men, all three built like navvies, all three towered over her, especially her husband, as he was the tallest. But she loved them all. They decided to go to a hotel for their anniversary. They shopped round and found an ideal one on the coast. They booked the bridal suite for themselves; even though they weren't just married, they still felt it. Everything was sorted through the hotel; they didn't have to do a thing. They booked into their room on the day, and it was just exquisite. They just had to christen the bed. Eric pulled Vicky onto it and kissed her tenderly. "I love you so very much. Always have and always will," he whispered as he looked down at her and began to undress her.

"I know, I have always known and I love you just as much," she said as she pulled at his clothes, wanting to get at his body.

"Yes, I have always known too." They were naked in no time and started to explore each other, driving each other mad with their touch. Eric gently slid upon her and they ended up making tender love to each other, relishing in the fact that they were together.

***

Today, Vicky and Eric are still as much in love as they always have been. They have now been married twenty-seven years and are still like a newly married couple. Vicky doesn't have nightmares all that often now, but she still does and when she does they wrack her scarred body, and she always ends up sobbing into Eric's chest, but her gentle giant is there to hold her tight and protect her always. David never married again; he still lives in the village and Tom still lives with him. They make a point of seeing Vicky every day, as they do with Eric at work. Even weekends you will find the four of them spending some quality time together. Tom is now twenty-three and still dotes on his Viddy. They eventually sold the Golden Thistle to the manager, Brian, who worked for them, and it is still doing okay. Eric's company is still going, with David and Tom helping to run it. Vicky's accountancy company was brought by some local businessman, and she is now just a housewife who dotes on her wonderful loving husband, and he loves it. Every time they are apart is a moment too long for either of them, and even to this day lunchtimes are special to them. It just goes to show that even though you can be scarred physically and mentally, true love will come through. And when you find it, cherish it. Eric and Vicky are proof it can happen.

THE END

Lightning Source UK Ltd.
Milton Keynes UK
UKOW041954030613

211702UK00002B/574/P